Big Book of
Things That Go

Huck Scarry's
Big Book of
Things That Go

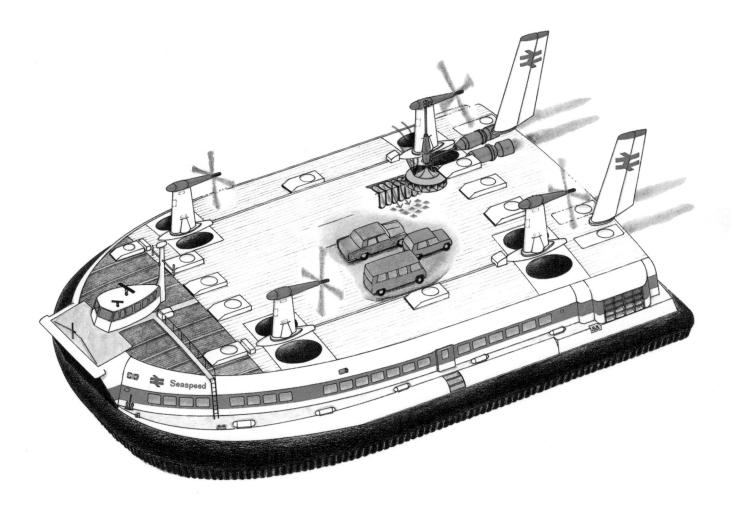

BARNES
&NOBLE
BOOKS
NEW YORK

Table of Contents

Copyright © 1984, 1985 Huck Scarry
Copyright © 1984, 1985 Arnoldo Mondadori Editore S.p.A., Milan
Revised edition copyright © 1992 Arnoldo Mondadori S.p.A., Milan
Lettering by Huck Scarry
This edition published by Barnes & Noble, Inc., by arrangement with Arnoldo Mondadori Editore S.p.A., Milan
© 1994 Barnes & Noble Books
All rights reserved. No part of this publication may be reproduced, stored in a retrieval system, or transmitted in any form or by any means, electronic, mechanical, photocopying, recording or otherwise, without the prior written permission of the publishers.
ISBN 1-56619-588-8
Printed and bound in Spain by Artes Graficas Toledo S.A.
D.L.TO:932-1994

Introduction

Those of us who live in large cities awaken each morning to a distant rumble, punctuated by the occasional nervous honking of horns. The sounds of traffic: the cars, buses, motor scooters and motorcycles, trolleys, trucks, and vans driven by people who got up early and are already out in the street and active, moving around, or perhaps are instead returning home after working the night shift.

People travel for necessity and for amusement, and they travel a great deal. They go to work or to school, out shopping or to visit friends, to restaurants, to vacation spots—and sometimes they just drive around. For some people, traveling is their business, such as truck drivers, taxi drivers, airplane pilots, sailors on ships, train engineers—and along with the engineers all the other people, from motormen to ticket takers and from station masters to conductors, who guarantee efficient rail transportation. And what about the transportation of goods? Only a very small portion of our world's raw materials, processed goods, manufactured products, and foodstuffs is used near the places where they are produced. A dense network of communication routes—by land, sea, and air—covers the surface of our planet, joining mines, oil wells, electricity plants, industries, factories, mills, deposits, storage dumps, warehouses, ocean and river ports, airports, towns, cities, and countries. The enormous network has links of various size that grow thicker at the major centers of production, distribution, and consumption and then thin out elsewhere.

If you take a close look at the objects in any one room of your home and reflect on the materials of which the objects are made and on all the many operations that had to be performed in different places, sometimes far away from one another, you will get at least a vague sense of the distance those objects had to travel before reaching your home. The same is true of the foods that appear every morning on the breakfast table, each of which came from a different place and had to perform quite a pilgrimage to reach your plate with the sole aim of pleasing your palate. The level of our well-being is in large measure related to our good fortune to be able to enjoy a wide variety of products that come to us from a wide variety of distant places.

This atlas tells the story of the means of transportation, showing how they evolved over the centuries and explaining the physical and technical laws that control them and make them work. The variety of means of transportation is surprisingly large, for they are responses to the changing needs of many centuries and are also the fruit of the natural instinct to improve everything.

But now all you have to do is turn the page to start on your way along an exciting journey through the wonderful world of transportation.

Things that Go

Can you imagine a world without transportation? Nothing would move. You would not be able to go see a friend. It would be impossible to go to the movies. You would be unable to go buy an ice cream! What a contrast to the world we live in today!

Indeed, every day, you go to school. How do you get there? Do your feet take you, or do you go by bus? Does your father drive to work, or does he ride a bike? And when Mother brings home groceries, how does she do it?

You see, we use transportation every day. We move about so much, on foot, by bicycle, by automobile, by bus, by train, that we hardly give these wonderful means of transport a second thought!

But do you really know how you walk? What keeps your bicycle from falling while you ride? How does a car's engine work? You don't know? Then turn the pages? Let's take a look and see what makes things go.

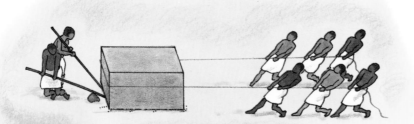

Friction increases as the weight of an object increases. Twice as much effort is required to move a weight of 20 pounds, as a weight of 10 pounds. That is why it takes tremendous energy to drag a stone block, weighing several tons, across the ground.

Much of the friction between rubbing surfaces can be eliminated by reducing the area of the sliding surfaces and improving them. Ancient Egyptian builders moved heavy stones on wooden sleds, reducing the friction surfaces to just the area of the sled runners. Friction could be further eliminated by laying wooden sleepers for the sled to be dragged over. The heat built up by the rubbing wooden surfaces was quenched by watering the sleepers in front of the sled.

Sled on track

Friction: Friend and Foe

Any objects moving against one another resist each other. This resistance is called friction. Because friction in many ways impedes movement, man, throughout history, has devised methods of overcoming it by using sleds, rollers, and wheels.

Friction can waste a lot of energy, building up heat between any moving parts. Tiny rollers or cylinders, called bearings, are placed liberally in machinery wherever friction is a problem, while lubricants such as oil and grease allow any sliding parts to move easily. Frequent lubrication is necessary to keep any machine in good, working order.

But friction is also a good friend. Without it, we would be unable to move! It allows us to adhere to the ground with our feet, letting us push ourselves forward. All rolling wheels adhere to some surface to move along. Friction also permits us to stop, once in motion. After the wheel, the brake is the most important part of any rolling vehicle!

Sled on rollers

Rolling friction is much less important than sliding friction, so progress can be greatly improved by placing mobile rollers under the sled. The final improvement would be, of course, to mount the sled on wheels. Rollers of one sort or another are found in almost all machinery, wherever two moving parts come into contact with one another. These are called bearings. The most common bearings are ball bearings and roller bearings, which allow two parts to glide past one another with a minimum of friction.

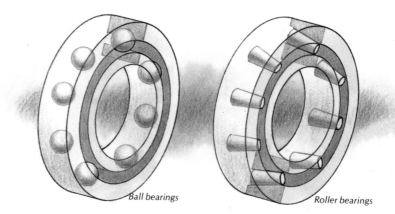

Ball bearings   *Roller bearings*

8

All the moving parts on a steam locomotive, such as the wheel cranks, had to be frequently oiled. Similarly an automobile engine must always have enough oil to lubricate it properly, allowing it to run with a minimum of friction.

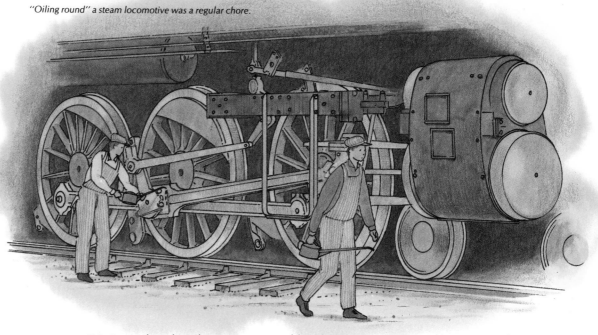

"Oiling round" a steam locomotive was a regular chore.

Friction is also a friend. Its resistance enables a locomotive wheel to advance on a rail, or a rubber tire to grip the road. These types of friction are called adhesion.

Lubricants are special liquids that are used to reduce friction between moving parts, allowing them to slide past each other on a low-friction liquid film. Gears, for instance, are often coated with grease, or housed in a bath of oil—two common lubricants.

Brake drum

High-friction material

Brake drum revolving with wheel

Brake shoes

Friction is applied against the drum, slowing it down.

Friction is necessary to make brakes work, causing them to slow or stop a vehicle. Shoes made of a high-friction material press against a disc or drum revolving with the wheel, building up resistance and bringing the vehicle to a halt.

Snow and ice have surfaces that offer little friction, making it easy to sled, to ski, or to skate. But the lack of friction on ice may make walking on it a painful experience!

9

Natural Locomotion

Imagine if you couldn't move! You could never go out or meet anyone. We tend to take movement for granted, yet it is one of the miracles of the animal world. Movement is a faculty all animals share, and nature has provided for it in a great variety of ways. Such movement is called natural locomotion, and some examples of this are shown below.

Walking

Concertina movement

Another type of axial locomotion is known as pedal movement, used by snails. The snail sets up waves of muscle contractions along the length of its lower body, moving backward, permitting the snail to move forward on a path of sticky mucus that it secretes beneath it.

Pedal locomotion

Land snail

Muscular foot with sole

Muscle waves

Secreted path of sticky mucus

Hundreds of tube feet under the arms.

Diagram of a tube foot

Starfish

Liquid

Foot extended   Foot contracted

Kangaroo

Peristaltic locomotion

Many animals have no arms or legs, and must use their whole body for movement. This type of movement is called axial locomotion. Snakes are some such animals, and one way they can advance is through what is known as concertina movement, because they squeeze and stretch like a concertina. Extending its head forward, the snake uses the rest of its body as an anchor. Once fully extended, it anchors with its head, pulling up the rest of its body, to start another "step" forward.

Starfish living on the ocean floor move about on hundreds of tiny tube feet carried under each of their "arms." These feet pull the animal along, extending, anchoring and contracting by means of a liquid the starfish pumps into the feet, filling or emptying them. This type of movement is described as peristaltic.

Saltation

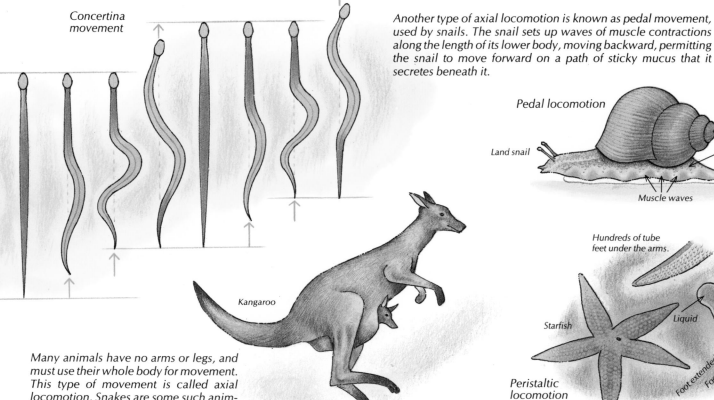

Frog

Frogs, kangaroos, rabbits and grasshoppers are just some of the animals that get about by thrusting their hindlegs powerfully, allowing them to jump ahead in bounds, often over considerable distances. This type of locomotion is called saltation.

The body pivots forward over the foot

A step

A stride

The foot is carried forward under the body

Animals which have arms and legs move about through appendicular locomotion. Humans fall into this category. One means we use to advance is called walking, and this is a cycle made up of two stages. First, the foot grips the ground (through friction), while the leg and body pivot forward over it. In the next stage, the body remains stationary, while the leg and foot swing forward. We call the advancement of one leg a step, while the cycle of advancement of all the animal's legs is known as a stride.

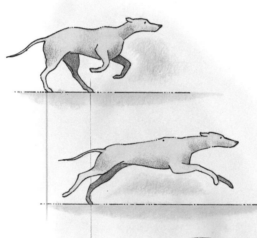

When running, the gait may become asymmetrical, as the animal powerfully launches itself through the air with its hind legs, carrying them well forward at touchdown.

Four-legged animals are the fastest on earth. Cheetahs are capable of reaching speeds of over 65 mph (105 kmh). The ostrich can attain speeds of 43 mph (70 kmh) on its two legs.

Trotting horse

The walking and trotting gaits of four-legged animals tend to be symmetrical, moving alternately from one pair of legs to the other.

Running dog

Here you can see one step of a trotting horse. Notice how it supports itself on opposite fore and hind legs, and with only two legs at a time. At the end of a step, for an instant, the horse doesn't touch the ground, landing on the opposite pair of fore and hindlegs.

Shaping a hot shoe on the anvil

Shoeing a horse

Horseshoes were made and fitted at the blacksmith's shop.

People wear shoes to protect their feet, as well as to improve their footing. Similarly, horses are shod with horseshoes, saving their hooves from injury and wear, while giving them a better hold on the ground. Although horseshoes have been made since ancient times, it was not until fairly recently that they were widely fitted.

Roman "hipposandal"

Frankish horseshoe

French horseshoe, 16th century

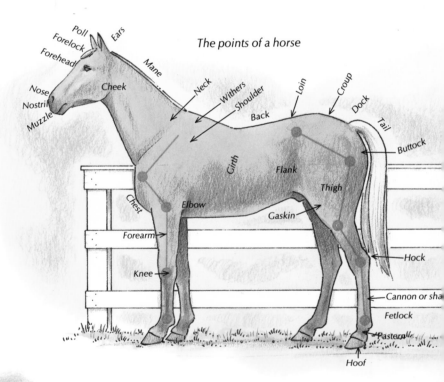

The points of a horse

Poll — Forelock — Forehead — Ears — Nose — Nostril — Muzzle — Cheek — Mane — Neck — Withers — Shoulder — Back — Loin — Croup — Dock — Tail — Buttock — Girth — Flank — Thigh — Chest — Elbow — Gaskin — Forearm — Hock — Knee — Cannon or shank — Fetlock — Pastern — Hoof

Horse and Harness

With the exception of the sail on ships and the water wheel on rushing streams, the harnessing of animals is one of the first means found by man of providing nonhuman power to do work.

In ancient times dogs, llamas and oxen were frequently used for pulling sleds and wheeled carts. Later, camels, asses, reindeer and finally horses were trained to be driven, and eventually ridden.

Indeed, until not much more than a century ago, horses still provided the only widespread, rapid source of power for land transportation. Since then, the "iron horse," or railway locomotive, and the automobile, with its "horse-power," have all but replaced the horse on the road. Today, horses are ridden or driven before carriages almost exclusively for pleasure and sport.

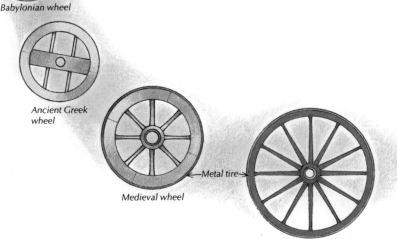

The wheel is certainly one of man's most useful inventions, as well as being one of his earliest. Perhaps derived from a rolling log or a tumbling stone, it greatly reduced the friction under any pulled load. It made it possible to transport heavier loads much faster and for greater distances.

Babylonian wheel

Ancient Greek wheel

Medieval wheel

Metal tire

18th-century wheel

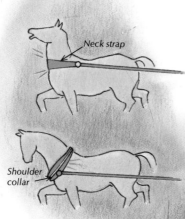

Neck strap

In ancient times harnesses consisted simply of a strap around the horse's neck. The harder the animal pulled, the more it choked.

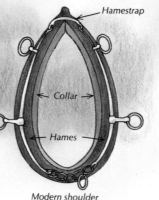

Shoulder collar

The modern harness we know today was introduced into Europe from Asia in about 800 A.D. It fits on the horse's shoulders without interfering with its breathing or circulation so the animal can use all its strength for pulling.

Hamestrap

Collar

Hames

Modern shoulder harness

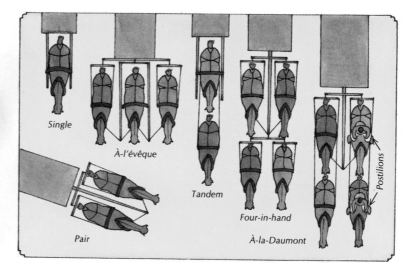

Single

À-l'évêque

Tandem

Four-in-hand

Pair

À-la-Daumont

Postilions

Over the centuries a variety of harnesses were designed for traction by one horse or several. Choice of one arrangement over another depended on the width of the road, speed, cost or the desire for elegance.

English saddle

Crown piece
Throatlatch
Browband
Cheek strap
Noseband
Pommel
Bit
Reins
Seat
Flap
Cantle
Pad
Stirrup leather
Girth
Stirrup

Western Saddle

Cantle
Seat
Pommel
Saddle strings
Flap
Flank strap
Stirrup
Front tie strap

Horses have been ridden for centuries using a variety of saddles. Today, the most popular riding saddle is the lightweight "English" saddle. In America the "Western" saddle was developed to enable cowboys to handle great herds of cattle from horseback. The pommel provided a means of securing the lasso when roping cattle.

Shaping the parts of the wheel rim, or "felly."

Driving the spokes into the hub

Fitting the fellies to the spokes

A metal tire and its wooden wheel

Fitting hot tire to the wheel

Cooling tire in water

The making of wheels was a fine craft that demanded a great deal of skill and precision. Here are the basic stages of the wheelmaking process.

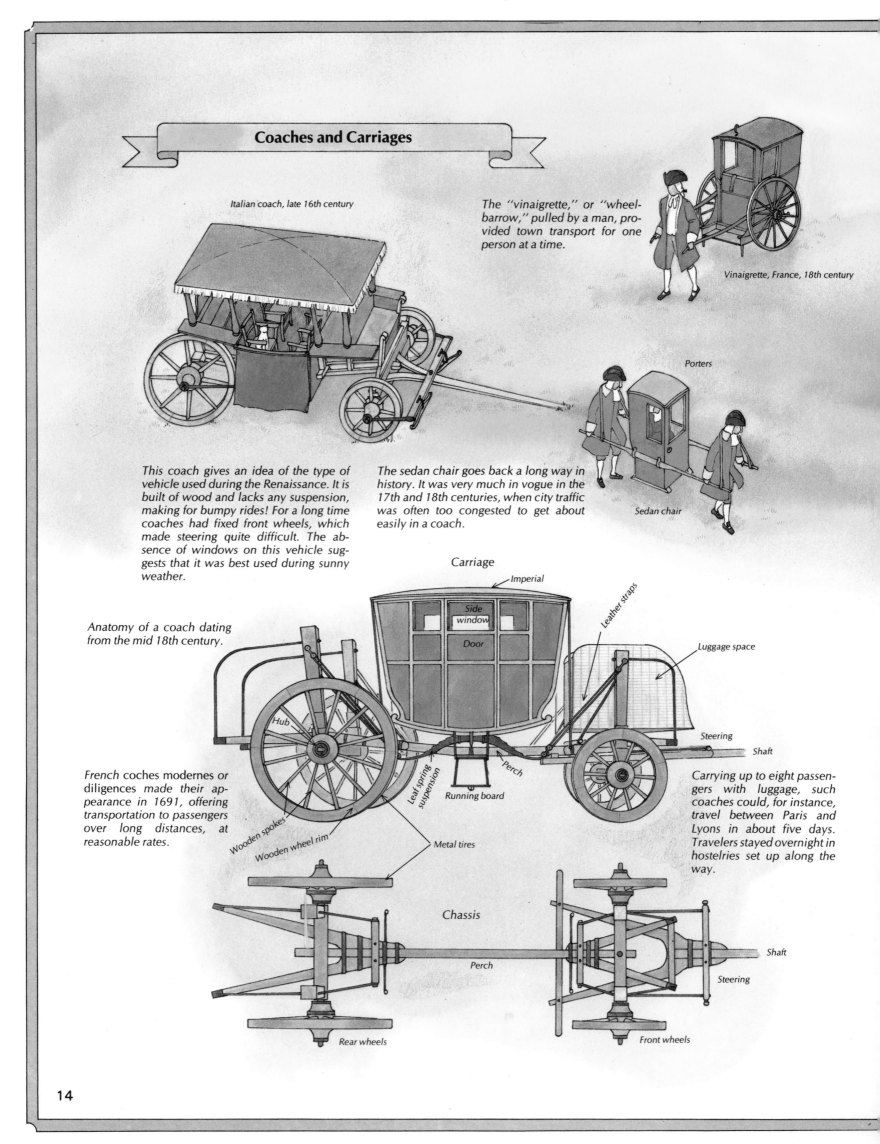

Coaches and Carriages

Italian coach, late 16th century

The "vinaigrette," or "wheelbarrow," pulled by a man, provided town transport for one person at a time.

Vinaigrette, France, 18th century

Porters

Sedan chair

This coach gives an idea of the type of vehicle used during the Renaissance. It is built of wood and lacks any suspension, making for bumpy rides! For a long time coaches had fixed front wheels, which made steering quite difficult. The absence of windows on this vehicle suggests that it was best used during sunny weather.

The sedan chair goes back a long way in history. It was very much in vogue in the 17th and 18th centuries, when city traffic was often too congested to get about easily in a coach.

Anatomy of a coach dating from the mid 18th century.

Carriage

Imperial

Side window

Door

Leather straps

Luggage space

Hub

Steering

Shaft

Perch

Leaf spring suspension

Running board

Wooden spokes

Wooden wheel rim

Metal tires

French coches modernes or diligences *made their appearance in 1691, offering transportation to passengers over long distances, at reasonable rates.*

Carrying up to eight passengers with luggage, such coaches could, for instance, travel between Paris and Lyons in about five days. Travelers stayed overnight in hostelries set up along the way.

Chassis

Shaft

Perch

Steering

Rear wheels

Front wheels

14

Conestoga wagon, American Colonies, 18th century

The Conestoga wagon takes its name from the town of Conestoga, Pennsylvania, where it was originally made. The Pioneer settlers used these peculiar boat-shaped wagons to cross the Appalachian mountains, via the Mohawk Trail, Cumberland Road, or Wilderness Road, in search of a new life in the "Wild West."

Horse's feed trough

The post chaise, which dates back to the mid 17th century, was a normal chair placed between two wheels and hitched up to a horse. In its day it was the most rapid and expensive means of transport for a single person. The word "post" in its name refers not to the post office but to the relay stations, where fresh horses could be exchanged for tired ones along the route. The post chaise was driven by a mounted postilion.

Postilion

Door folds forward to enter

Splashboard

Post chaise, France, mid 18th century

Driver

Postman

Shoe, to park without rolling

"Coupé-Landau" postal stagecoach, Switzerland, 1850

Horse-drawn vehicles were built to a variety of designs, to suit different purposes. Here are some classic examples.

Stagecoaches were the forerunners of the intercity buses and trains of today. In many countries the post office organized stagecoach services carrying both passengers and mail. One of the most famous alpine routes was from Lucerne in Switzerland to Milan in Italy, via the St. Gotthard pass. By stagecoach this nonstop trip took 24 hours. Today, by automobile, the same drive is done in a few hours.

Drag   Dogcart   Omnibus   Post chaise   Carrosse

Berlin   Berlin Coupé   Phaeton   Landau   Break   Cabriolet

Machines

We live in a world of machines. Every day we travel in cars, ride in elevators and speak on telephones. Machines help us to do work, or to move around. Almost all machines are made up of moving parts. All moving parts can be defined as one or another very simple element that transforms energy and controls the direction of motion. We call such elements the simple machines. These are the lever, wheel and axle, pulley, wedge, inclined plane and screw. Let's see how machines help us in our everyday life.

A first-class lever

Levers are of three types, called first, second and third-class levers.

First-class levers have the fulcrum placed between the load and the effort. Seesaws are typical first-class levers.

A second-class lever

Second-class levers have the load placed between the fulcrum and the effort arm. Wheelbarrows are typical second-class levers.

The wheel and axle is also a first-class lever. Here the load lies on the radius of the axle, the effort is at the crank and the fulcrum lies in the axis of rotation or hub. A pulley wheel is a first-class lever whose load and effort arms are of unequal distance, giving a mechanical advantage thus making it easier to lift heavy weights.

A third-class lever

The third-class lever has the load at one end, the fulcrum at the other, and the effort in between. The driving axle and wheel of an automobile is a typical third-class lever. Such levers require a lot of effort to move the load, since the load travels farther than the effort.

A wedge is a simple machine that magnifies the effort put into it from above, in a sideways direction. Nails and hatchets are well-known wedges. A screw is a wedge wrapped around a cylinder, while the inclined plane, almost too simple to look like a machine, is actually a wedge where the effort is applied directly to the load.

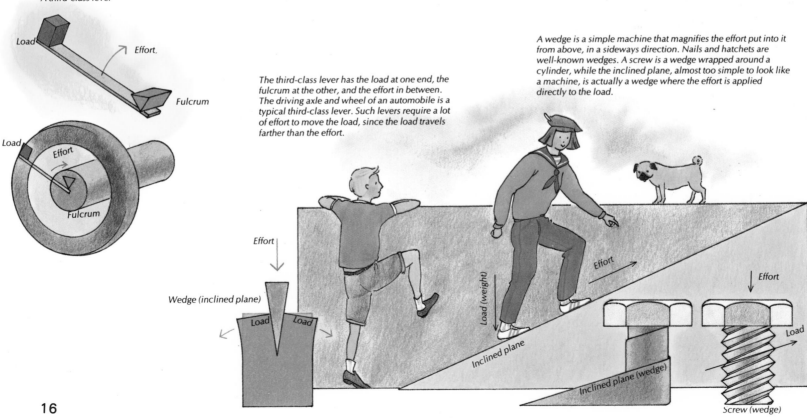

16

The efficiency of a machine is the ratio between the amount of energy put into it, and the amount of energy it puts out. No machine is 100 percent efficient, as all machines use up some of the input energy through friction between moving parts. This energy is lost as heat.

The mechanical advantage of a machine is the ratio between the force put into a machine, and the force it puts out. It is basically the amplification of force.

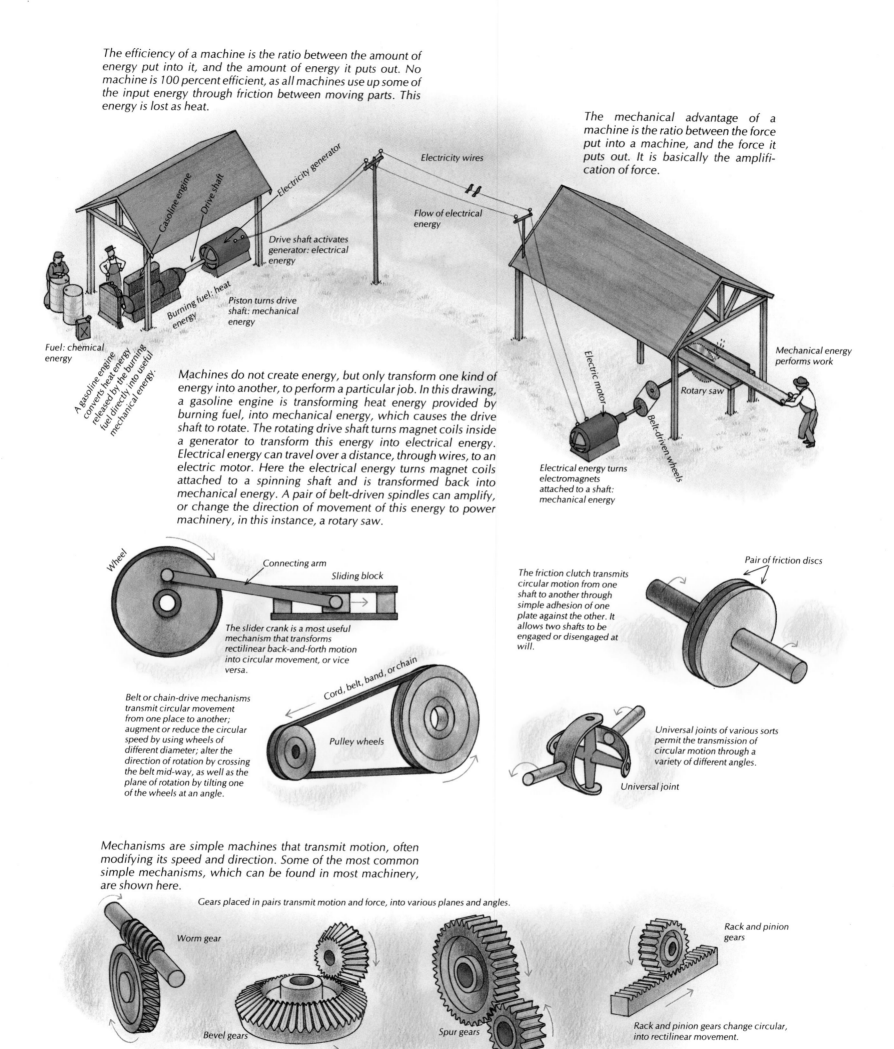

Electricity generator

Gasoline engine

Drive shaft

Electricity wires

Drive shaft activates generator: electrical energy

Flow of electrical energy

Burning fuel; heat energy

Piston turns drive shaft: mechanical energy

Fuel: chemical energy

A gasoline engine converts heat energy released by the burning fuel directly into useful mechanical energy.

Electric motor

Mechanical energy performs work

Rotary saw

Belt-driven wheels

Electrical energy turns electromagnets attached to a shaft: mechanical energy

Machines do not create energy, but only transform one kind of energy into another, to perform a particular job. In this drawing, a gasoline engine is transforming heat energy provided by burning fuel, into mechanical energy, which causes the drive shaft to rotate. The rotating drive shaft turns magnet coils inside a generator to transform this energy into electrical energy. Electrical energy can travel over a distance, through wires, to an electric motor. Here the electrical energy turns magnet coils attached to a spinning shaft and is transformed back into mechanical energy. A pair of belt-driven spindles can amplify, or change the direction of movement of this energy to power machinery, in this instance, a rotary saw.

Wheel

Connecting arm

Sliding block

The slider crank is a most useful mechanism that transforms rectilinear back-and-forth motion into circular movement, or vice versa.

Pair of friction discs

The friction clutch transmits circular motion from one shaft to another through simple adhesion of one plate against the other. It allows two shafts to be engaged or disengaged at will.

Belt or chain-drive mechanisms transmit circular movement from one place to another; augment or reduce the circular speed by using wheels of different diameter; alter the direction of rotation by crossing the belt mid-way, as well as the plane of rotation by tilting one of the wheels at an angle.

Cord, belt, band, or chain

Pulley wheels

Universal joints of various sorts permit the transmission of circular motion through a variety of different angles.

Universal joint

Mechanisms are simple machines that transmit motion, often modifying its speed and direction. Some of the most common simple mechanisms, which can be found in most machinery, are shown here.

Gears placed in pairs transmit motion and force, into various planes and angles.

Worm gear

Bevel gears

Spur gears

Rack and pinion gears

Rack and pinion gears change circular, into rectilinear movement.

Worm gears and bevel gears change the direction and speed of rotation.

Spur gears change the speed of rotation and intensity of force.

Anatomy of a Bicycle

Bicycles are among the simplest and best known mechanical vehicles. They comprise a variety of simple machines all of which are easily identifiable. How many of them can you find on your bicycle?

Bicycles were also among the first mechanical vehicles to be developed and their simplicity of design, lightness and easy maintenance still make them one of the most popular means of transport today.

The very first bicycle was invented by Baron Karl Drais von Sauerbronn, which he demonstrated in Paris in 1818. Big, heavy and cumbersome to steer, it was propelled by simply swinging one's legs along the ground, or by coasting downhill. In spite of its clumsiness, it soon became popular, and was known as a "Draisienne" in honor of its inventor.

Baron Drais' "Draisienne"

Spinning top

What keeps a bicycle upright? It is, in fact, the same force that acts on a spinning top, or on a gyroscope, and is called gyroscopic inertia. The rapidly spinning bicycle wheels set up a strong centrifugal force that defies any other . . . even that of gravity. But if you slow the wheels down the force disappears, and you will start to wobble. Similarly, a quickly spinning top stands up by itself, but as it slows down, it wobbles and finally falls over.

The "dérailleur" gear-change mechanism operates through a small lever and cable, which acts on a parallelogram device at the rear hub. This moves sprockets, which guide the roller chain from side to side, allowing the chain to engage with a number of toothed driving sprockets attached to the rear wheel hub. Most rear wheel dérailleurs carry five gear sprockets. The bigger sprockets are the low gears, while the smaller ones are the high gears. Very often, the driving sprocket carries a second, smaller one. Five speeds at the rear, and two up front give the rider ten gear ratios to choose from.

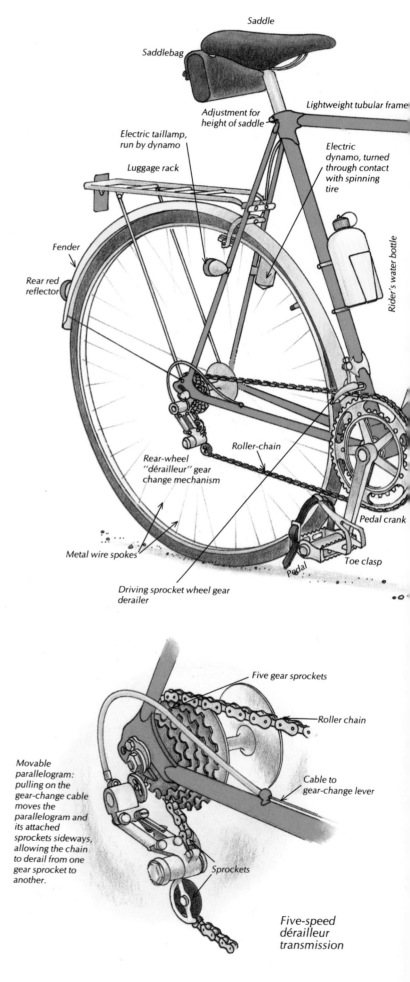

Saddle

Saddlebag

Adjustment for height of saddle

Lightweight tubular frame

Electric taillamp, run by dynamo

Electric dynamo, turned through contact with spinning tire

Luggage rack

Rider's water bottle

Fender

Rear red reflector

Rear-wheel "dérailleur" gear change mechanism

Roller-chain

Pedal crank

Metal wire spokes

Pedal

Toe clasp

Driving sprocket wheel gear derailer

Five gear sprockets

Roller chain

Movable parallelogram: pulling on the gear-change cable moves the parallelogram and its attached sprockets sideways, allowing the chain to derail from one gear sprocket to another.

Cable to gear-change lever

Sprockets

Five-speed dérailleur transmission

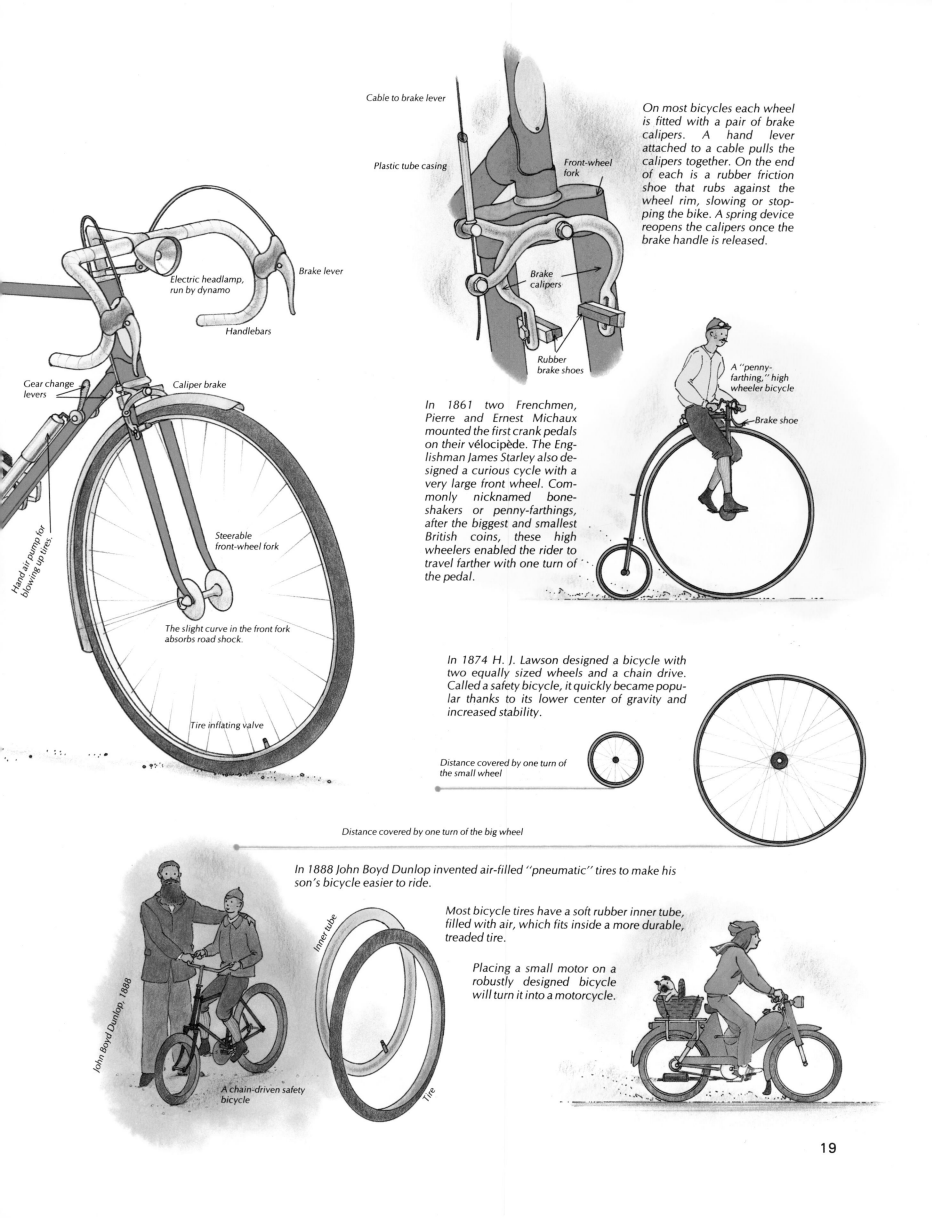

Cable to brake lever

Plastic tube casing

Front-wheel fork

On most bicycles each wheel is fitted with a pair of brake calipers. A hand lever attached to a cable pulls the calipers together. On the end of each is a rubber friction shoe that rubs against the wheel rim, slowing or stopping the bike. A spring device reopens the calipers once the brake handle is released.

Brake calipers

Rubber brake shoes

Electric headlamp, run by dynamo

Brake lever

Handlebars

Gear change levers

Caliper brake

Hand air pump for blowing up tires.

Steerable front-wheel fork

The slight curve in the front fork absorbs road shock.

Tire inflating valve

A "penny-farthing," high wheeler bicycle

Brake shoe

In 1861 two Frenchmen, Pierre and Ernest Michaux mounted the first crank pedals on their vélocipède. The Englishman James Starley also designed a curious cycle with a very large front wheel. Commonly nicknamed boneshakers or penny-farthings, after the biggest and smallest British coins, these high wheelers enabled the rider to travel farther with one turn of the pedal.

In 1874 H. J. Lawson designed a bicycle with two equally sized wheels and a chain drive. Called a safety bicycle, it quickly became popular thanks to its lower center of gravity and increased stability.

Distance covered by one turn of the small wheel

Distance covered by one turn of the big wheel

In 1888 John Boyd Dunlop invented air-filled "pneumatic" tires to make his son's bicycle easier to ride.

John Boyd Dunlop, 1888

A chain-driven safety bicycle

Inner tube

Tire

Most bicycle tires have a soft rubber inner tube, filled with air, which fits inside a more durable, treaded tire.

Placing a small motor on a robustly designed bicycle will turn it into a motorcycle.

19

Baron Drais von Sauerbronn's "Draisienne," Germany, 1817

Nicéphore Niepce made this steerable vélocifère in 1818.

Steerable front wheel

The German Baron Drais von Sauerbronn patented his steerable "Draisienne" in 1817. In 1818, when he first presented his invention to the public in Paris, he was met with ridicule. Today he is considered the father of the bicycle.

Comte de Sivrac's célerifère, France, 1791

Steerable front wheel

Niepce vélocifère, France, 1818

The Comte de Sivrac is believed to be the inventor of the very first "pedestrian hobby-horse," which he pushed about Paris with his feet.

A number of unusual designs for cycles appeared in the second half of the 19th century. Among these was the "dicycle," patented by E. C. T. Otto between 1879 and 1881. Steering was controlled by slackening one drive belt, thus permitting the wheels to turn at different speeds.

Otto "dicycle," Great Britain, 1880

Drive belt, slackened for steering

Anatomy of a motorcycle

Handlebars, with clutch, accelerator and brake handles

Rear-wheel shock absorber

Oil tank

Gas tank

Fender

Saddle

Headlight

Horn

Rubber fork boots housing shock absorbers

Tail and stop light

License plate

Brake

Brake rod

Engine

Muffler

Gearbox

Brake

Foot rest

Foot gear shift

Brake cable

Kick stand

Aermacchi 350cc Ala-blu

Smaller-engined scooters and lightweight motorbikes are popular around the world today.

Scooter

Engine

Motorcycle

Exhaust

In 1885 Gottlieb Daimler built this motorized bicycle, which he called a "riding car." It is a forerunner of the motorcycle.

Gottlieb Daimler's "riding-car," Germany, 1885

Michaux gas-powered vélocipède, France, 1869

Pierre and Ernest Michaux fitted a small gasoline engine to one of their vélocipèdes in 1869, giving them credit for making the first motorcycle.

20

Macmillan's push pedal hobby-horse, Great Britain, 1839

Push pedal

A Scottish blacksmith, Kirkpatrick Macmillan, built the first bicycle powered by pedals, which the rider pushed back and forth with his feet.

Brake

Crank pedals

Michaux vélocipède, France, 1860s

The coachbuilder Pierre Michaux and his son Ernest were the first to attach crank pedals to the wheel of a bicycle, which they successfully rode in Paris in 1861. The Michaux family began manufacturing vélocipèdes, which became very popular.

In 1870 the Englishman James Starley, who was manufacturing Michaux vélocipèdes in England, set about to improve the vehicle. He reduced their weight, and enlarged the front wheel, enabling faster speeds to be attained.

Starley bicycle, Great Britain, 1872

Harry John Lawson's "bicyclette," Great Britain, 1879

Chain drive

H. J. Lawson made the first chain-driven bicycle, making the wheels smaller, and thus putting the rider closer to the ground. Lawson called his cycle a bicyclette, but it soon became known as the safety bicycle, while high wheelers became ordinaries. Safeties made cycling easier for everybody.

Racing high wheeler, 1884

High wheelers were often raced by dashing young men. The diameter of the driving wheel was limited only by the length of the rider's legs.

Pneumatic tires

John Boyd Dunlop's pneumatic tires on a safety bicycle, Great Britain, 1888

The Scotsman John Boyd Dunlop, looking for a way to soften the ride on his son's bicycle, fitted air-filled tires to it. This not only made riding softer, but faster. Today, the invention of pneumatic tires is attributed to Dunlop.

Lightweight racing bicycle (with no brakes) following a quintuplet team of trainers, late 19th century.

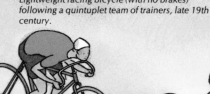

Bicycle races, either outdoors on the road, or indoors on special oval tracks, quickly became popular. Champions on lightweight machines trained for races by pacing themselves behind a powerful team of trainers.

A major development in bicycle design came in 1962, when the Englishman Alexander Moulton invented a bicycle with a very low center of gravity and excellent suspension.

Luggage rack

Shock absorber

Flexible suspension

Moulton bicycle, Great Britain, 1962

Steam Power

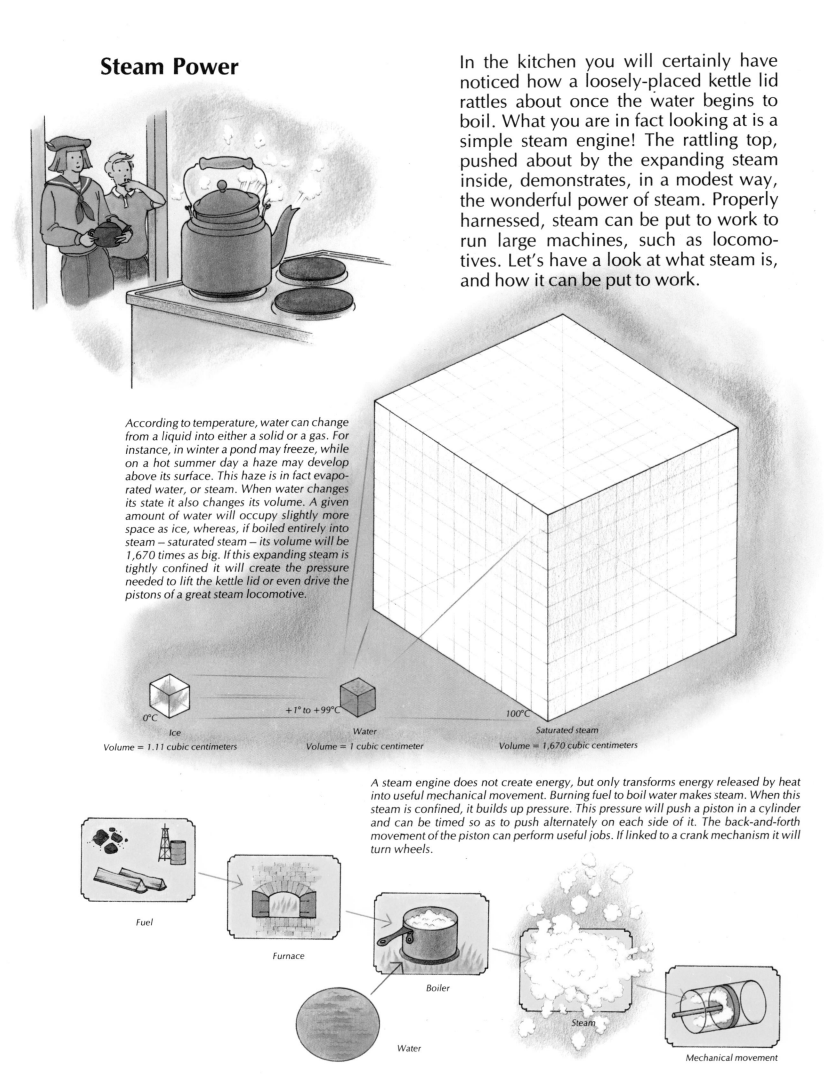

In the kitchen you will certainly have noticed how a loosely-placed kettle lid rattles about once the water begins to boil. What you are in fact looking at is a simple steam engine! The rattling top, pushed about by the expanding steam inside, demonstrates, in a modest way, the wonderful power of steam. Properly harnessed, steam can be put to work to run large machines, such as locomotives. Let's have a look at what steam is, and how it can be put to work.

According to temperature, water can change from a liquid into either a solid or a gas. For instance, in winter a pond may freeze, while on a hot summer day a haze may develop above its surface. This haze is in fact evaporated water, or steam. When water changes its state it also changes its volume. A given amount of water will occupy slightly more space as ice, whereas, if boiled entirely into steam – saturated steam – its volume will be 1,670 times as big. If this expanding steam is tightly confined it will create the pressure needed to lift the kettle lid or even drive the pistons of a great steam locomotive.

0°C
Ice
Volume = 1.11 cubic centimeters

+1° to +99°C
Water
Volume = 1 cubic centimeter

100°C
Saturated steam
Volume = 1,670 cubic centimeters

A steam engine does not create energy, but only transforms energy released by heat into useful mechanical movement. Burning fuel to boil water makes steam. When this steam is confined, it builds up pressure. This pressure will push a piston in a cylinder and can be timed so as to push alternately on each side of it. The back-and-forth movement of the piston can perform useful jobs. If linked to a crank mechanism it will turn wheels.

Fuel

Furnace

Boiler

Water

Steam

Mechanical movement

22

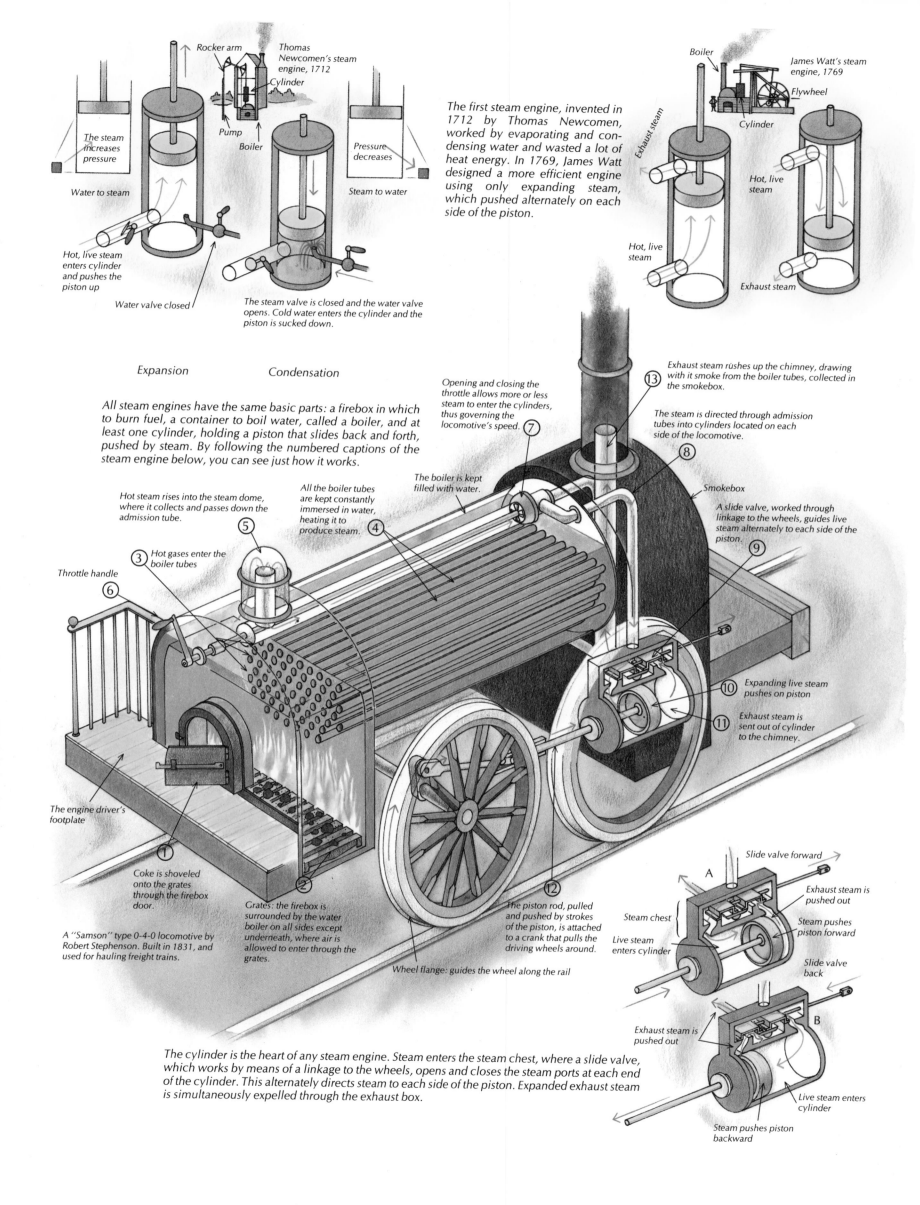

Rocker arm

Thomas Newcomen's steam engine, 1712

Cylinder

Pump

Boiler

The steam increases pressure

Water to steam

Pressure decreases

Steam to water

Hot, live steam enters cylinder and pushes the piston up

Water valve closed

The steam valve is closed and the water valve opens. Cold water enters the cylinder and the piston is sucked down.

Expansion

Condensation

Boiler

James Watt's steam engine, 1769

Flywheel

Cylinder

Exhaust steam

Hot, live steam

Hot, live steam

Exhaust steam

The first steam engine, invented in 1712 by Thomas Newcomen, worked by evaporating and condensing water and wasted a lot of heat energy. In 1769, James Watt designed a more efficient engine using only expanding steam, which pushed alternately on each side of the piston.

All steam engines have the same basic parts: a firebox in which to burn fuel, a container to boil water, called a boiler, and at least one cylinder, holding a piston that slides back and forth, pushed by steam. By following the numbered captions of the steam engine below, you can see just how it works.

Hot steam rises into the steam dome, where it collects and passes down the admission tube.

All the boiler tubes are kept constantly immersed in water, heating it to produce steam.

Opening and closing the throttle allows more or less steam to enter the cylinders, thus governing the locomotive's speed.

The boiler is kept filled with water.

Exhaust steam rushes up the chimney, drawing with it smoke from the boiler tubes, collected in the smokebox.

The steam is directed through admission tubes into cylinders located on each side of the locomotive.

Smokebox

A slide valve, worked through linkage to the wheels, guides live steam alternately to each side of the piston.

Hot gases enter the boiler tubes

Throttle handle

Expanding live steam pushes on piston

Exhaust steam is sent out of cylinder to the chimney.

The engine driver's footplate

Coke is shoveled onto the grates through the firebox door.

A "Samson" type 0-4-0 locomotive by Robert Stephenson. Built in 1831, and used for hauling freight trains.

Grates: the firebox is surrounded by the water boiler on all sides except underneath, where air is allowed to enter through the grates.

The piston rod, pulled and pushed by strokes of the piston, is attached to a crank that pulls the driving wheels around.

Wheel flange: guides the wheel along the rail

The cylinder is the heart of any steam engine. Steam enters the steam chest, where a slide valve, which works by means of a linkage to the wheels, opens and closes the steam ports at each end of the cylinder. This alternately directs steam to each side of the piston. Expanded exhaust steam is simultaneously expelled through the exhaust box.

Slide valve forward

A

Exhaust steam is pushed out

Steam chest

Steam pushes piston forward

Live steam enters cylinder

Slide valve back

Exhaust steam is pushed out

B

Steam pushes piston backward

Live steam enters cylinder

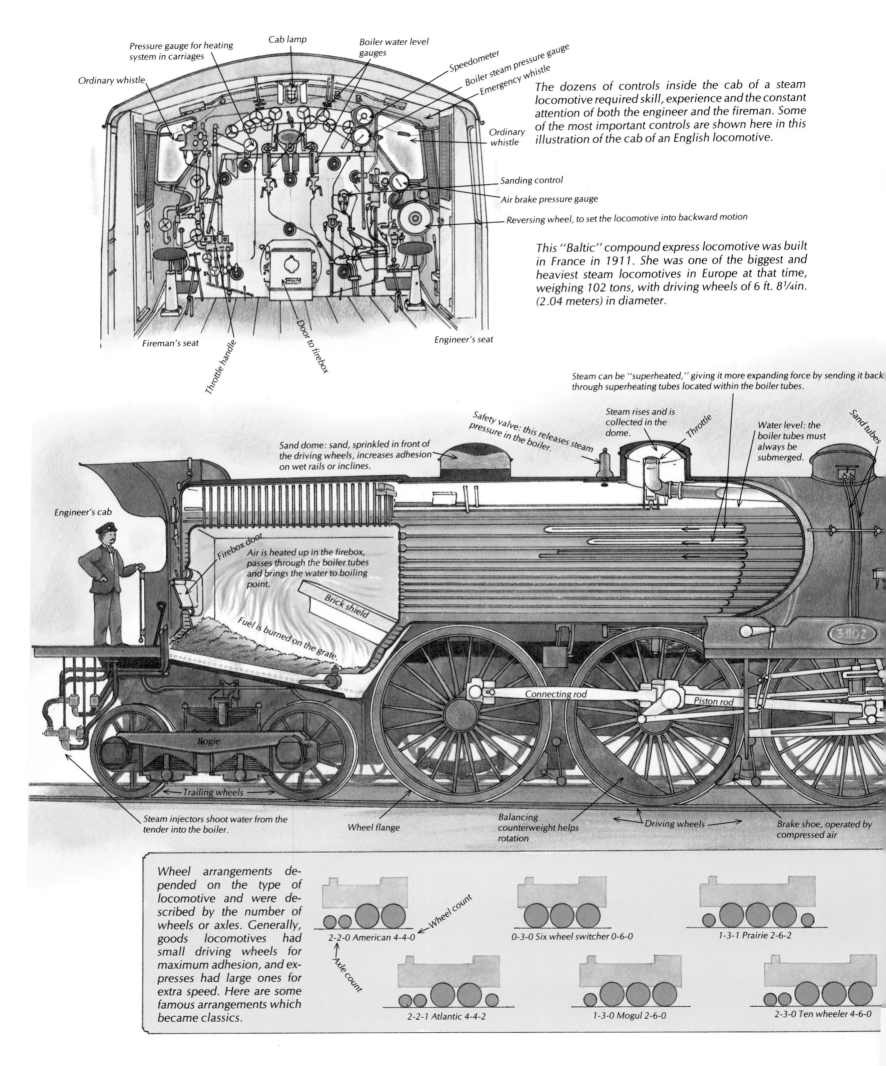

Pressure gauge for heating system in carriages

Cab lamp

Boiler water level gauges

Speedometer

Boiler steam pressure gauge

Emergency whistle

Ordinary whistle

Ordinary whistle

The dozens of controls inside the cab of a steam locomotive required skill, experience and the constant attention of both the engineer and the fireman. Some of the most important controls are shown here in this illustration of the cab of an English locomotive.

Sanding control

Air brake pressure gauge

Reversing wheel, to set the locomotive into backward motion

This "Baltic" compound express locomotive was built in France in 1911. She was one of the biggest and heaviest steam locomotives in Europe at that time, weighing 102 tons, with driving wheels of 6 ft. 8¼in. (2.04 meters) in diameter.

Fireman's seat

Throttle handle

Door to firebox

Engineer's seat

Steam can be "superheated," giving it more expanding force by sending it back through superheating tubes located within the boiler tubes.

Safety valve: this releases steam pressure in the boiler.

Steam rises and is collected in the dome.

Throttle

Water level: the boiler tubes must always be submerged.

Sand tubes

Sand dome: sand, sprinkled in front of the driving wheels, increases adhesion on wet rails or inclines.

Engineer's cab

Firebox door

Air is heated up in the firebox, passes through the boiler tubes and brings the water to boiling point.

Brick shield

Fuel is burned on the grate.

3.1102

Connecting rod

Piston rod

Bogie

Trailing wheels

Steam injectors shoot water from the tender into the boiler.

Wheel flange

Balancing counterweight helps rotation

Driving wheels

Brake shoe, operated by compressed air

Wheel arrangements depended on the type of locomotive and were described by the number of wheels or axles. Generally, goods locomotives had small driving wheels for maximum adhesion, and expresses had large ones for extra speed. Here are some famous arrangements which became classics.

Wheel count

Axle count

2-2-0 American 4-4-0

0-3-0 Six wheel switcher 0-6-0

1-3-1 Prairie 2-6-2

2-2-1 Atlantic 4-4-2

1-3-0 Mogul 2-6-0

2-3-0 Ten wheeler 4-6-0

Steam Locomotives

There is no more exciting sight than that of a steam locomotive in action. With its puffing smoke and hissing steam it almost seems to be alive. Even today, long after electric and diesel locomotives have replaced them, no one would dispute their fascination and beauty. Let's take a look inside and try and understand why.

Water tank

A steam locomotive burns either coal, wood, or oil to heat water to make steam. All the fuel and water had to be carried with the locomotive, so often a special tender was pulled along behind. Large locomotives consumed tremendous amounts of water, so frequent stops to take on water were necessary on every trip.

Steam is sent through admission tubes to the cylinders.

Drawn from an exhibit in the National Railway Museum, Mulhouse, France

Hot gases from the boiler tubes enter the smokebox, and escape up the chimney.

A door allows for regular cleaning of the boiler tubes and the smokebox.

Exhaust steam is expelled through the chimney.

Lantern

Buffer

Coupling

Leading wheels

The slide valve directs live steam to each side of the piston.

Partially expanded steam is sent from the cylinders to other low-pressure cylinders located between the wheels, powering a second set of pistons.

Steam admission tubes to the cylinders

Air brake compressors

Coal and water tender

The Walschaerts valve gear controls the synchronization of movement between the slide valves and pistons, as well as forward and reverse movement of the locomotive.

2-3-1 Pacific 4-6-2

1-4-0 Consolidation 2-8-0

2-4-1 Mountain 4-8-2

1-5-1 Santa Fe 2-10-2

2-3-2 Hudson or Baltic 4-6-4

1-4-1 Mikado 2-8-2

1-5-0 Decapod 2-10-0

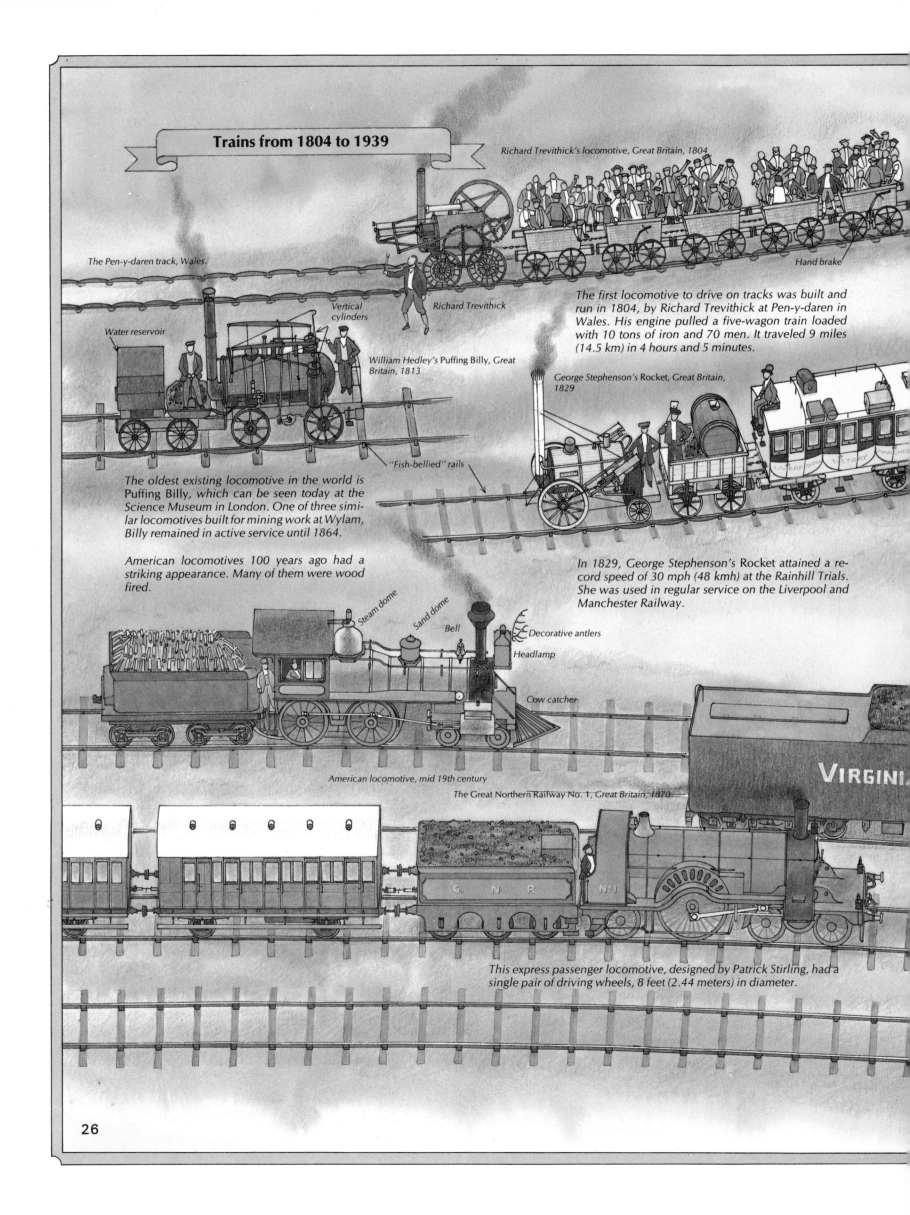

Trains from 1804 to 1939

Richard Trevithick's locomotive, Great Britain, 1804

Hand brake

The Pen-y-daren track, Wales.

Vertical cylinders

Richard Trevithick

The first locomotive to drive on tracks was built and run in 1804, by Richard Trevithick at Pen-y-daren in Wales. His engine pulled a five-wagon train loaded with 10 tons of iron and 70 men. It traveled 9 miles (14.5 km) in 4 hours and 5 minutes.

Water reservoir

William Hedley's Puffing Billy, Great Britain, 1813

George Stephenson's Rocket, Great Britain, 1829

"Fish-bellied" rails

The oldest existing locomotive in the world is Puffing Billy, which can be seen today at the Science Museum in London. One of three similar locomotives built for mining work at Wylam, Billy remained in active service until 1864.

American locomotives 100 years ago had a striking appearance. Many of them were wood fired.

In 1829, George Stephenson's Rocket attained a record speed of 30 mph (48 kmh) at the Rainhill Trials. She was used in regular service on the Liverpool and Manchester Railway.

Steam dome

Sand dome

Bell

Decorative antlers

Headlamp

Cow catcher

American locomotive, mid 19th century

The Great Northern Railway No. 1, Great Britain, 1870.

VIRGINIA

G N R No 1

This express passenger locomotive, designed by Patrick Stirling, had a single pair of driving wheels, 8 feet (2.44 meters) in diameter.

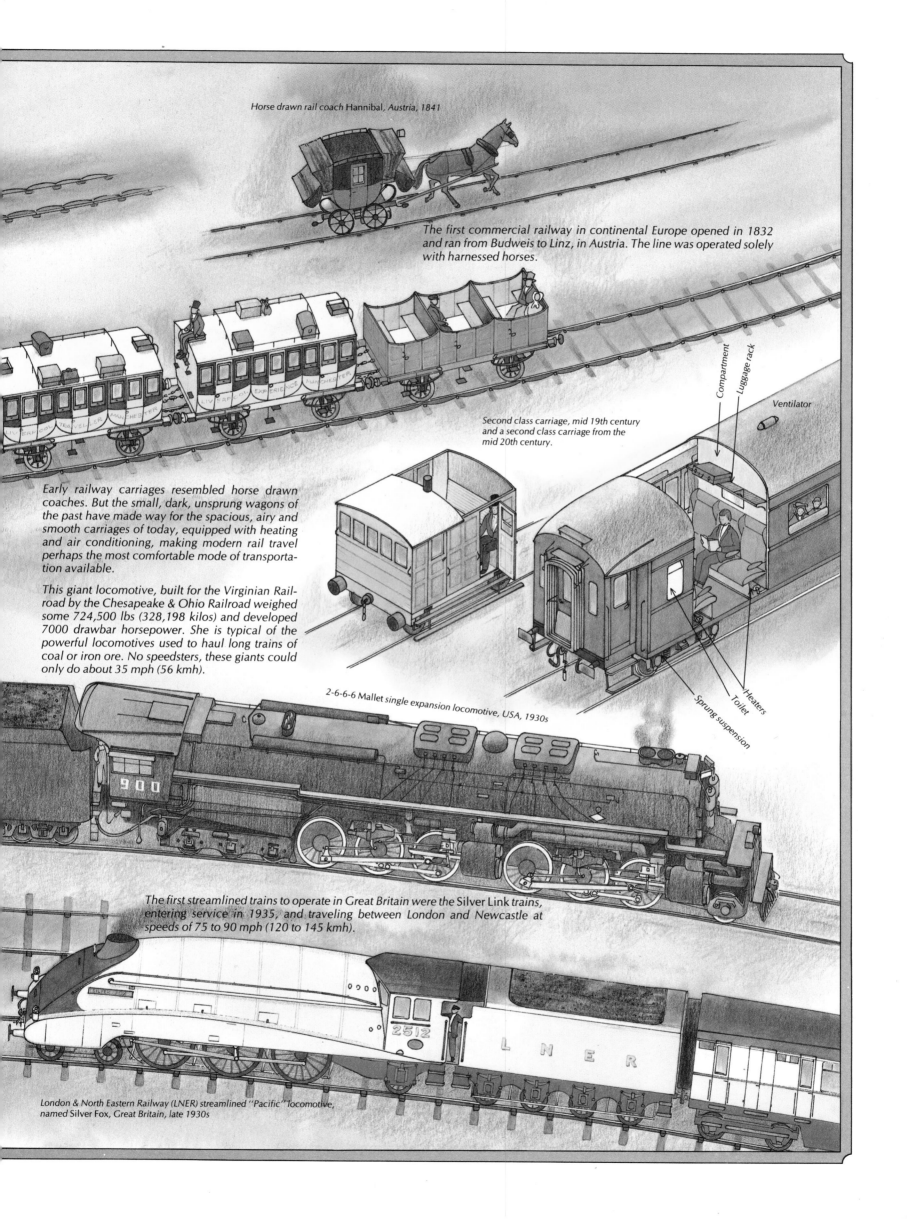

Horse drawn rail coach Hannibal, Austria, 1841

The first commercial railway in continental Europe opened in 1832 and ran from Budweis to Linz, in Austria. The line was operated solely with harnessed horses.

Second class carriage, mid 19th century and a second class carriage from the mid 20th century.

Compartment

Luggage rack

Ventilator

Early railway carriages resembled horse drawn coaches. But the small, dark, unsprung wagons of the past have made way for the spacious, airy and smooth carriages of today, equipped with heating and air conditioning, making modern rail travel perhaps the most comfortable mode of transportation available.

This giant locomotive, built for the Virginian Railroad by the Chesapeake & Ohio Railroad weighed some 724,500 lbs (328,198 kilos) and developed 7000 drawbar horsepower. She is typical of the powerful locomotives used to haul long trains of coal or iron ore. No speedsters, these giants could only do about 35 mph (56 kmh).

2-6-6-6 Mallet single expansion locomotive, USA, 1930s

Heaters

Toilet

Sprung suspension

900

The first streamlined trains to operate in Great Britain were the Silver Link trains, entering service in 1935, and traveling between London and Newcastle at speeds of 75 to 90 mph (120 to 145 kmh).

2512

L N E R

London & North Eastern Railway (LNER) streamlined "Pacific" locomotive, named Silver Fox, Great Britain, late 1930s

Magic in a Magnet, a Wizard in a Wire

Electricity, one of our most versatile, adaptable, efficient, powerful, and most widely used energy sources, is also one of the most difficult to understand.

In our everyday life, just about every machine we use gets its power from electricity. In land transportation, its best application has been to electric locomotives. But before we look at these, let's try to understand the basic principles of electric power.

Magnets have a strange, invisible force enabling them to pick up bits of metal without hooks, or glue. Two bar magnets, placed one way, will stick to each other, while placed in another, push apart.

All magnets have two poles, which we call North and South. Unlike magnetic poles attract one another, while like poles repel.

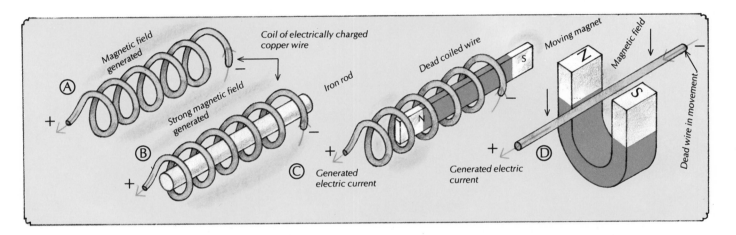

Magnetic field generated

Coil of electrically charged copper wire

Strong magnetic field generated

Iron rod

Dead coiled wire

Moving magnet

Magnetic field

Generated electric current

Generated electric current

Dead wire in movement

Magnetism and electricity are closely related. In A, an electric current passing through a piece of coiled wire will cause a magnetic field to be formed around it. Placing a rod of iron inside the coil, as in B, will strengthen this magnetic field considerably. (This is an electromagnet.) In C, an electric current can be generated in a dead coil of wire, by moving a magnet through it. Similarly, a piece of dead wire, *moved through a magnetic field, will become charged with electric current, D. An electric current will only be made as long as there is the proper movement between the wire, and the magnetic field. This is how electricity is generated in big power plants. The phenomenon by which a magnetic field generates electricity, and vice versa, is called electromagnetic induction.*

What is electric current?

Simplified diagram of an atom:

. . .of a conductor. The electron has a loose orbit.

. . .of an insulator. The electron has a tight orbit.

You have doubtlessly already seen a diagram of an atom. A large mass in the center is called the nucleus, and this is orbited by a number of smaller electrons. In some materials, like silver, iron, or copper, the electrons' orbits are very loose. Under the influence of magnetism, these electrons can actually be tugged out of their orbit, and drift to another atom. This drift of electrons from one atom to the next is electric current. Materials which allow such drift are called conductors.

Atoms of a conductor with their loose orbiting electrons

Influenced by a magnetic field, drifting electrons make an electric current.

Electric current can, of course, also be generated through chemical reactions, which is what happens in batteries.

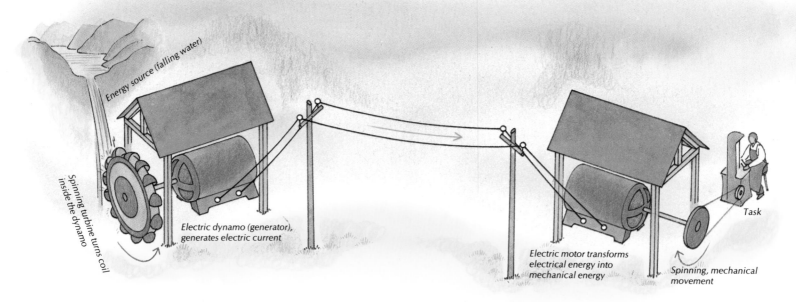

Energy source (falling water)

Spinning turbine turns coil inside the dynamo

Electric dynamo (generator), generates electric current

Electric motor transforms electrical energy into mechanical energy

Spinning, mechanical movement

Task

Electricity is a most useful and convenient form of energy and is highly efficient, losing little of its power through friction or heat. Using a turbine, it can be generated from a variety of energy sources, be it falling water, or expanding steam. The current can then be transported over long distances by wires to an electric motor, which changes the current back into a mechanical spinning movement, ready to do any job.

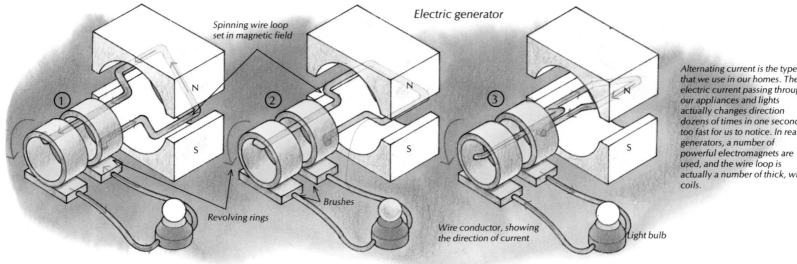

Electric generator

Spinning wire loop set in magnetic field

① ② ③

N S

Revolving rings

Brushes

Wire conductor, showing the direction of current

Light bulb

Alternating current is the type that we use in our homes. The electric current passing through our appliances and lights actually changes direction dozens of times in one second – too fast for us to notice. In real generators, a number of powerful electromagnets are used, and the wire loop is actually a number of thick, wire coils.

In this simplified diagram, we can see how electricity is generated in an "alternating current" generator. A wire loop, whose ends are attached to a pair of rotating metal rings, is placed inside a magnetic field. When the loop is set in motion, by an outside force (a turbine), an electric current is generated in it. Brushes in contact with the rings, pick up the current, which is sent through wires to the light bulb (or an electric motor). In 1, the loop in movement cuts the lines of magnetic force, and current is generated in one direction. When the loop is parallel to the magnetic field, as in 2, the magnetic lines of force are not being cut, so no current is generated. As the loop continues its turn, in 3, the lines of force are cut again, but the current has reversed its direction.

Electric motor

Winding

Electromagnets

Armature

N S

Commutator

Brushes

An electric motor works like a generator, but the effects are reversed. Using a brush, electric current is picked up from wires by a revolving "commutator," which sends it through a loop, called the armature, placed in a magnetic field. By means of another brush, the current then passes into a series of wires wound around a pair of electromagnets, called the winding, causing the magnets to work, pulling and pushing on the spinning armature. The armature, of course, is also charged, but the split commutator, as it turns, constantly changes the armature's polarity, so that it always spins in the same direction. A spinning shaft attached to the armature can be hooked up to do any job.

First electric locomotive, built by Siemens & Halske, Germany, 1879. (Run at the Berlin Industrial Trade Exhibition, 1879.)

The first electric railway locomotive was designed as an attraction at the Berlin Industrial Trade Exhibition of 1879. It pulled three carriages holding six persons each. Running along a circular track 300 meters long, it had a top speed of some 7 kmh (4 mph).

29

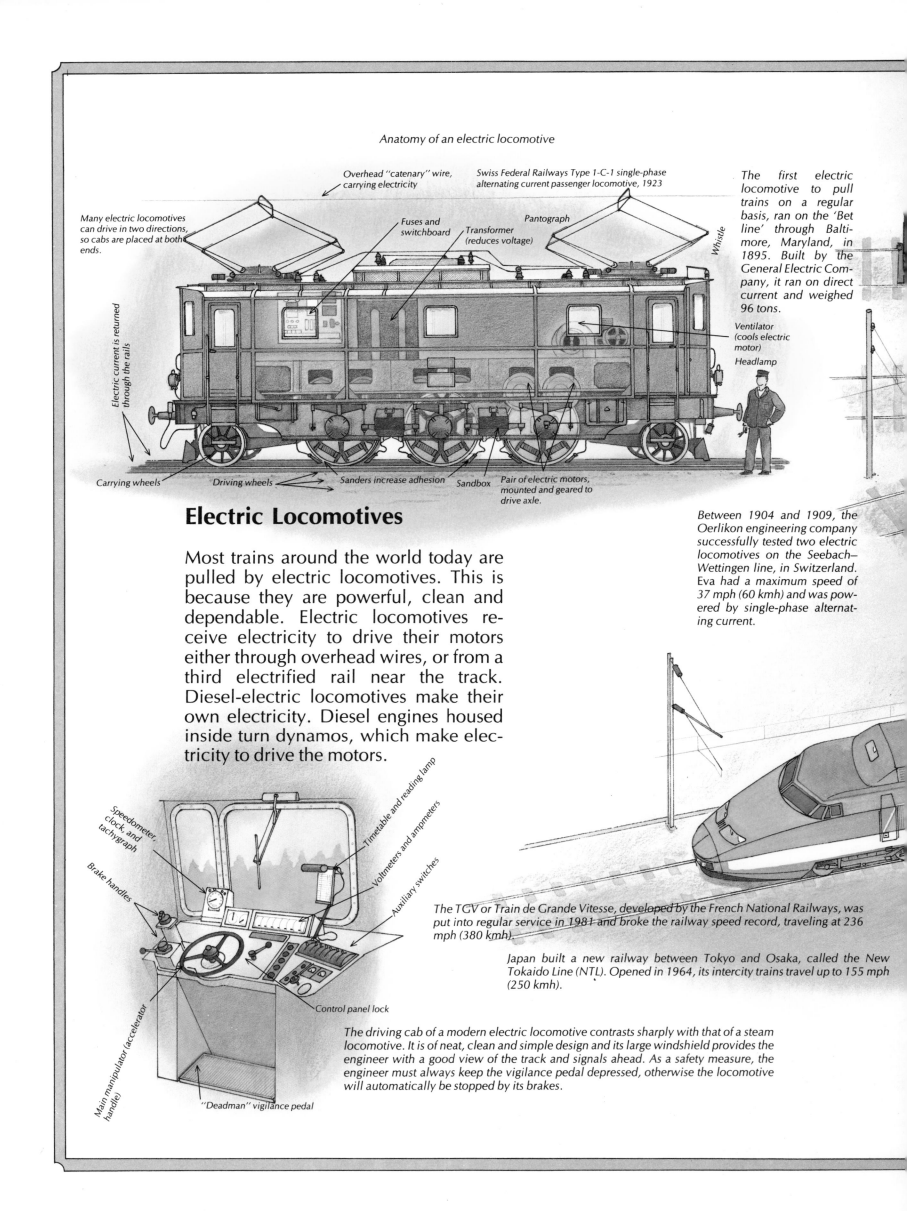

Overhead ''catenary'' wire, carrying electricity

Swiss Federal Railways Type 1-C-1 single-phase alternating current passenger locomotive, 1923

Many electric locomotives can drive in two directions, so cabs are placed at both ends.

Fuses and switchboard

Transformer (reduces voltage)

Pantograph

Whistle

The first electric locomotive to pull trains on a regular basis, ran on the 'Bet line' through Baltimore, Maryland, in 1895. Built by the General Electric Company, it ran on direct current and weighed 96 tons.

Electric current is returned through the rails

Ventilator (cools electric motor)

Headlamp

Carrying wheels

Driving wheels

Sanders increase adhesion

Sandbox

Pair of electric motors, mounted and geared to drive axle.

Electric Locomotives

Most trains around the world today are pulled by electric locomotives. This is because they are powerful, clean and dependable. Electric locomotives receive electricity to drive their motors either through overhead wires, or from a third electrified rail near the track. Diesel-electric locomotives make their own electricity. Diesel engines housed inside turn dynamos, which make electricity to drive the motors.

Between 1904 and 1909, the Oerlikon engineering company successfully tested two electric locomotives on the Seebach–Wettingen line, in Switzerland. Eva had a maximum speed of 37 mph (60 kmh) and was powered by single-phase alternating current.

Speedometer, clock, and tachygraph

Timetable and reading lamp

Voltmeters and ampmeters

Auxiliary switches

Brake handles

Control panel lock

Main manipulator (accelerator handle)

''Deadman'' vigilance pedal

The TGV or Train de Grande Vitesse, developed by the French National Railways, was put into regular service in 1981 and broke the railway speed record, traveling at 236 mph (380 kmh).

Japan built a new railway between Tokyo and Osaka, called the New Tokaido Line (NTL). Opened in 1964, its intercity trains travel up to 155 mph (250 kmh).

The driving cab of a modern electric locomotive contrasts sharply with that of a steam locomotive. It is of neat, clean and simple design and its large windshield provides the engineer with a good view of the track and signals ahead. As a safety measure, the engineer must always keep the vigilance pedal depressed, otherwise the locomotive will automatically be stopped by its brakes.

Electric locomotive "No. 1," Baltimore & Ohio Railroad, USA, 1895

Electric locomotive, Burgdorf-Thun Railway, Switzerland, 1899

The Brown–Boveri Company built this electric locomotive, the first in regular operation in Europe. She was capable of 22 mph (36 kmh) with passenger trains and of 12 mph (18 kmh) with freight.

The first electric underground railway began operation in London, in 1890.

Crompton electric locomotive and Padded cell passenger car, City & South London Railway, Great Britain, 1900

Eva Ce 4/4 Type, Seebach-Wettingen Railway, Switzerland, 1904

Crocodile Ce 6/8 II Type freight locomotive, Switzerland, 1920

The Swiss Federal Railways ran powerful locomotives like this one on the steep St. Gotthard line. Known as "Crocodiles," they weighed 126 tons and had a top speed of 46 mph (75 kmh).

TGV, France, 1981

NTL train, Japan, 1964

Electric locomotives, like steam locomotives, are designated by letters and numbers indicating pairs of driving wheels (A, B, C, D) and pairs of carrying wheels (1, 2, 3, 4). Here are some typical examples.

B-B   Connecting rod   C

C-C   1-C-1   2-D-2

Proceed with Caution

Many trains use the same line of track, often in opposite directions. It is therefore very important to have a complex system of signals to prevent accidents. Nowadays, these systems are entirely automatic and work electronically, making accidents virtually impossible.

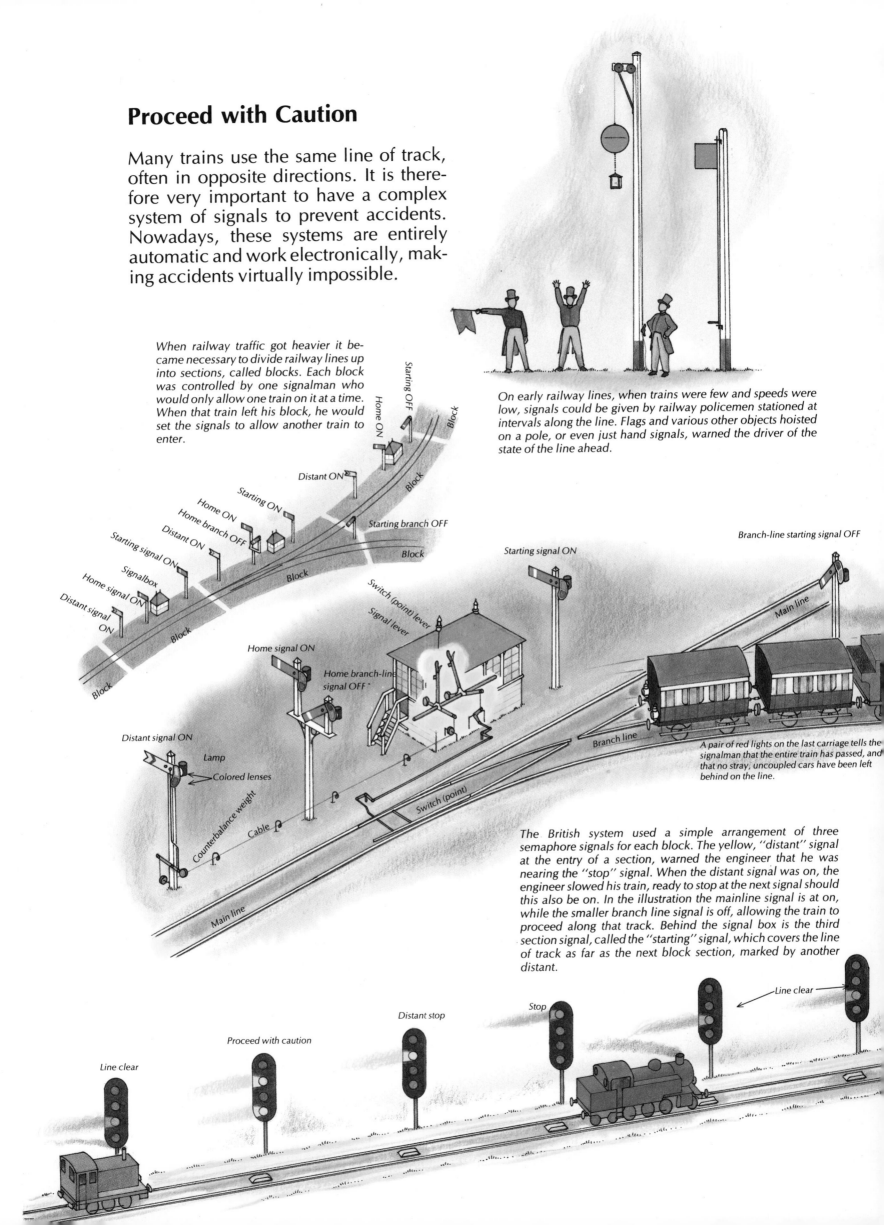

When railway traffic got heavier it became necessary to divide railway lines up into sections, called blocks. Each block was controlled by one signalman who would only allow one train on it at a time. When that train left his block, he would set the signals to allow another train to enter.

On early railway lines, when trains were few and speeds were low, signals could be given by railway policemen stationed at intervals along the line. Flags and various other objects hoisted on a pole, or even just hand signals, warned the driver of the state of the line ahead.

Starting OFF

Home ON

Block

Block

Distant ON

Home ON

Starting ON

Home branch OFF

Distant ON

Starting branch OFF

Block

Starting signal ON

Signalbox

Home signal ON

Distant signal ON

Block

Block

Home signal ON

Home branch-line signal OFF

Switch (point) lever

Signal lever

Starting signal ON

Branch-line starting signal OFF

Main line

Distant signal ON

Lamp

Colored lenses

Counterbalance weight

Cable

Switch (point)

Branch line

Main line

A pair of red lights on the last carriage tells the signalman that the entire train has passed, and that no stray, uncoupled cars have been left behind on the line.

The British system used a simple arrangement of three semaphore signals for each block. The yellow, "distant" signal at the entry of a section, warned the engineer that he was nearing the "stop" signal. When the distant signal was on, the engineer slowed his train, ready to stop at the next signal should this also be on. In the illustration the mainline signal is at on, while the smaller branch line signal is off, allowing the train to proceed along that track. Behind the signal box is the third section signal, called the "starting" signal, which covers the line of track as far as the next block section, marked by another distant.

Line clear

Proceed with caution

Distant stop

Stop

Line clear

Line clear

Tablet collecting arm

Tablet

Single line tablet post

Running several trains on a single line of track demands extra caution. In former times, an engineer may have been required to carry a token with him, called a tablet. This was picked up at the beginning of the line, and deposited at the end, where another driver could pick it up, and enter the line. In theory as only one train at a time could carry the tablet, a collision, was impossible.

Here are some typical semaphore signals used for many years in different countries around the world. Today, most semaphores have been replaced by electric searchlight signals.

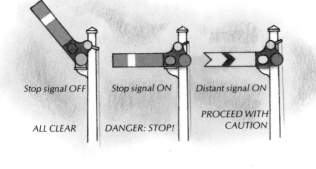

Stop signal OFF

ALL CLEAR

Stop signal ON

DANGER: STOP!

Distant signal ON

PROCEED WITH CAUTION

British semaphore signals, called quadrant semaphores because they tilt within quarters of circles, were either red stop signals, or swallow-tailed, yellow distant signals. When the arm was horizontal, the signal was on. If the arm was tilted either up, or down, then it was off.

German distant signal at caution

Sempahore signals took a variety of shapes in different countries. Although each country had its own system, they all worked equally well towards the same end—safety on the line!

Swiss stop signal at stop,

. . . . . . and at all clear

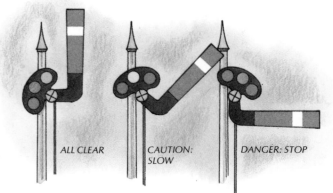

ALL CLEAR

CAUTION: SLOW

DANGER: STOP

This American semaphore shows three positions.

Most railway lines today are equipped with automatic block signaling, activated by the passing trains themselves. The line is divided up into numerous block sections, each one protected by a multiposition searchlight signal. Next to the signal on the track is a magnetic "crocodile," sensitive to the passage of trains. When a locomotive passes over a crocodile, the signal turns to red (stop), closing access to the track behind the train. As the train passes the next crocodile, the first signal changes to yellow (caution), until the train is far enough away for that signal to return to green (all clear), permitting another train to pass.

Should a driver not obey a stop warning along the line, a magnetic "crocodile" placed between the rails next to the signal will transmit a warning to the cab. A blinking box and loud horn tell the driver to wake up and put on the brakes!

Shoe

"Crocodile" magnet

Cogs and Cables

Because of the poor adhesion of metal wheels to metal rails locomotives cannot easily climb steep inclines. In order to overcome this a number of different solutions have been devised.

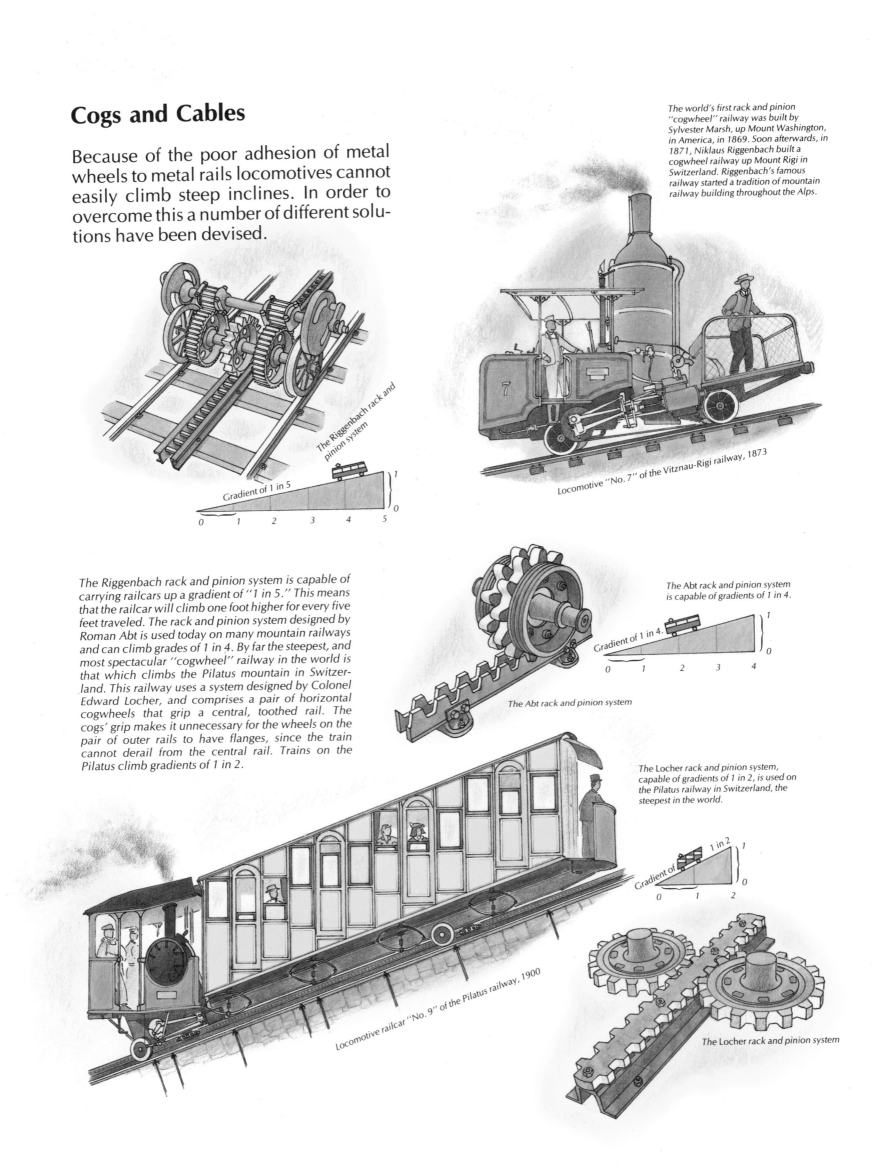

The world's first rack and pinion "cogwheel" railway was built by Sylvester Marsh, up Mount Washington, in America, in 1869. Soon afterwards, in 1871, Niklaus Riggenbach built a cogwheel railway up Mount Rigi in Switzerland. Riggenbach's famous railway started a tradition of mountain railway building throughout the Alps.

The Riggenbach rack and pinion system

Gradient of 1 in 5

Locomotive "No. 7" of the Vitznau-Rigi railway, 1873

The Riggenbach rack and pinion system is capable of carrying railcars up a gradient of "1 in 5." This means that the railcar will climb one foot higher for every five feet traveled. The rack and pinion system designed by Roman Abt is used today on many mountain railways and can climb grades of 1 in 4. By far the steepest, and most spectacular "cogwheel" railway in the world is that which climbs the Pilatus mountain in Switzerland. This railway uses a system designed by Colonel Edward Locher, and comprises a pair of horizontal cogwheels that grip a central, toothed rail. The cogs' grip makes it unnecessary for the wheels on the pair of outer rails to have flanges, since the train cannot derail from the central rail. Trains on the Pilatus climb gradients of 1 in 2.

The Abt rack and pinion system is capable of gradients of 1 in 4.

Gradient of 1 in 4.

The Abt rack and pinion system

The Locher rack and pinion system, capable of gradients of 1 in 2, is used on the Pilatus railway in Switzerland, the steepest in the world.

Gradient of 1 in 2

Locomotive railcar "No. 9" of the Pilatus railway, 1900

The Locher rack and pinion system

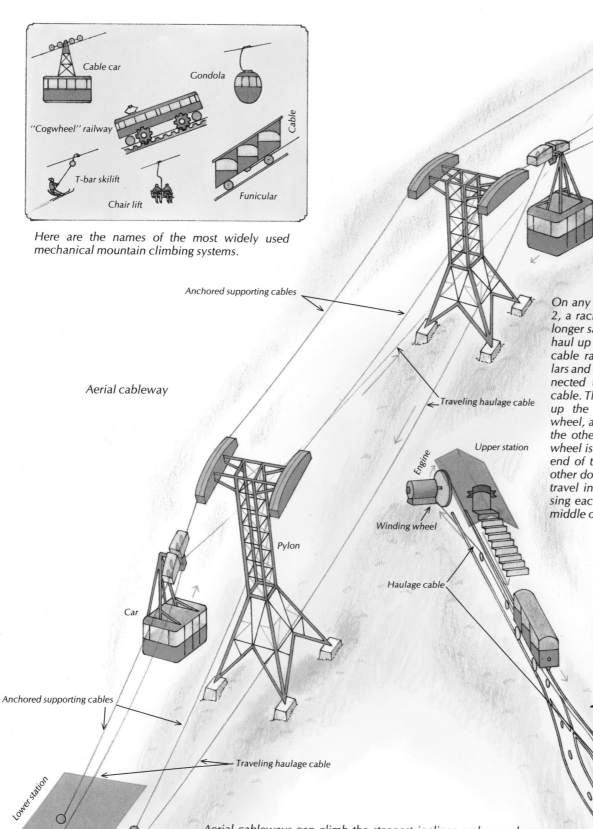

Cable car

Gondola

"Cogwheel" railway

Cable

T-bar skilift

Chair lift

Funicular

Here are the names of the most widely used mechanical mountain climbing systems.

Upper station

Anchored supporting cables

Aerial cableway

Traveling haulage cable

On any gradient steeper than 1 in 2, a rack and pinion system is no longer safe. The only solution is to haul up a railcar on a cable. Such cable railways are called funiculars and consist of two railcars connected to the ends of one long cable. The cable runs from one car, up the line, over the winding wheel, and down the line again to the other car. When the winding wheel is set in motion, it pulls one end of the cable up, sending the other down, so the railcars always travel in opposite directions, passing each other at the loop at the middle of the line.

Upper station

Engine

Winding wheel

Haulage cable

Pylon

Car

Funicular railway

Anchored supporting cables

Traveling haulage cable

Loop for passing

Lower station

Car

Winding wheel

Aerial cableways can climb the steepest inclines and span deep valleys in a single or series of swoops. A railway without rails, the car is suspended from an anchored supporting cable that it rides over on rollers. A haulage cable, similar to that of a funicular, runs from one car, around a winding wheel, to the other car, so that in motion, one car moves up while the other goes down. Aerial cableways are less expensive to build and operate than conventional railways, for there is no track to lay, and less to maintain. They are the joy of hikers and of skiers the world over!

Lower station

Admission, Compression, Ignition, Exhaust

If you have ever looked under the hood of a car, you will doubtlessly have been amazed by the complex picture of twisted pipes, coils of stringy wire, wandering rubber hoses and oddly shaped boxes. It is strange to think that something that looks so awkward can actually propel a car! Yet, for all its complexity at first view, the gasoline engine does in fact work in a very simple way. Let's take a quick look and see how it goes.

The engine is the heart of an automobile. How complicated it looks! Although it is made up of many, different parts, each one does a small, simple job, which helps the engine work smoothly. Of course, should one small piece cease to function, the whole engine may not work. It is little wonder that breakdowns are commonplace! Fortunately, often a small repair to one part will suffice to bring the engine to life again.

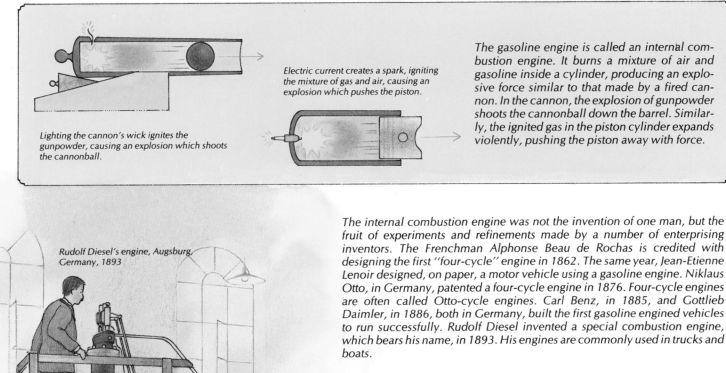

Lighting the cannon's wick ignites the gunpowder, causing an explosion which shoots the cannonball.

Electric current creates a spark, igniting the mixture of gas and air, causing an explosion which pushes the piston.

The gasoline engine is called an internal combustion engine. It burns a mixture of air and gasoline inside a cylinder, producing an explosive force similar to that made by a fired cannon. In the cannon, the explosion of gunpowder shoots the cannonball down the barrel. Similarly, the ignited gas in the piston cylinder expands violently, pushing the piston away with force.

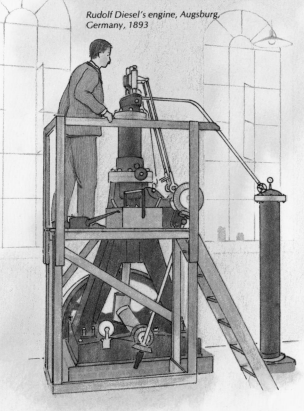

Rudolf Diesel's engine, Augsburg, Germany, 1893

The internal combustion engine was not the invention of one man, but the fruit of experiments and refinements made by a number of enterprising inventors. The Frenchman Alphonse Beau de Rochas is credited with designing the first "four-cycle" engine in 1862. The same year, Jean-Etienne Lenoir designed, on paper, a motor vehicle using a gasoline engine. Niklaus Otto, in Germany, patented a four-cycle engine in 1876. Four-cycle engines are often called Otto-cycle engines. Carl Benz, in 1885, and Gottlieb Daimler, in 1886, both in Germany, built the first gasoline engined vehicles to run successfully. Rudolf Diesel invented a special combustion engine, which bears his name, in 1893. His engines are commonly used in trucks and boats.

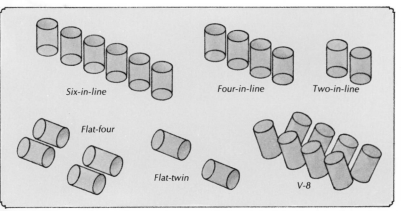

Six-in-line   Four-in-line   Two-in-line

Flat-four   Flat-twin   V-8

Different types of gasoline engines are distinguished by the number, size, and arrangement of the cylinders. Here are some common engine cylinder arrangements.

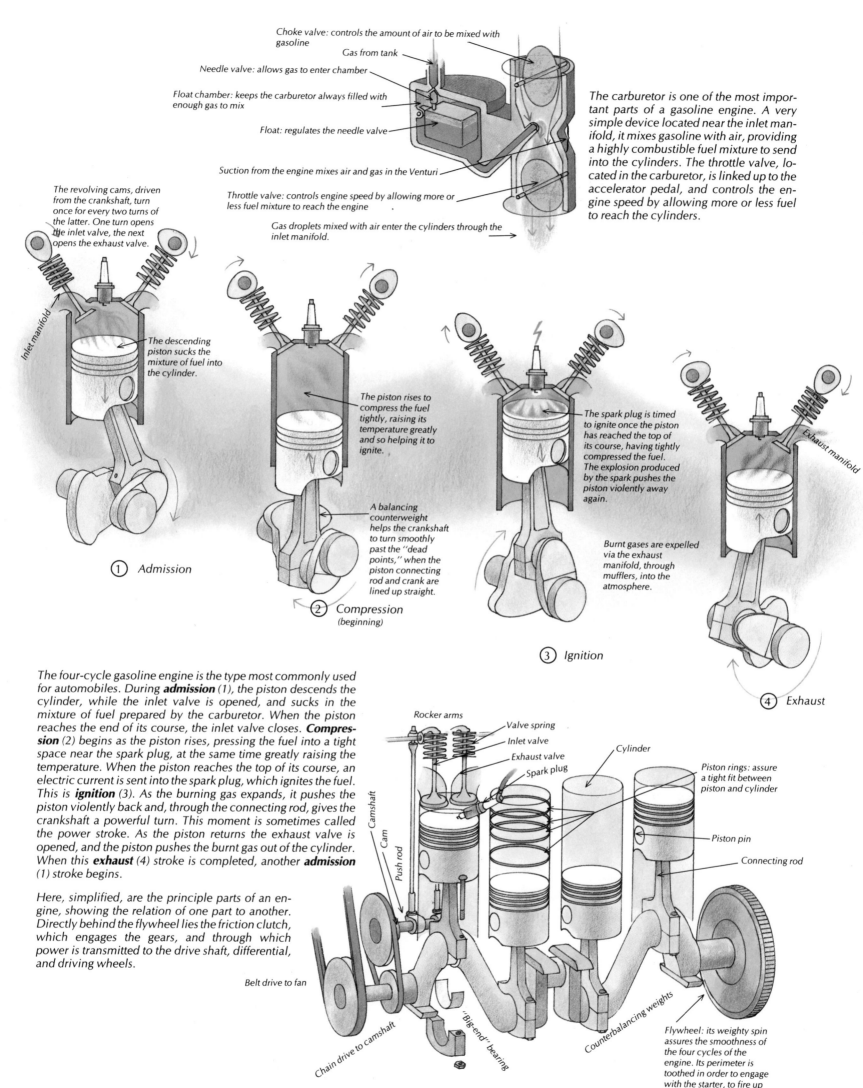

Choke valve: controls the amount of air to be mixed with gasoline

Gas from tank

Needle valve: allows gas to enter chamber

Float chamber: keeps the carburetor always filled with enough gas to mix

Float: regulates the needle valve

Suction from the engine mixes air and gas in the Venturi

Throttle valve: controls engine speed by allowing more or less fuel mixture to reach the engine

Gas droplets mixed with air enter the cylinders through the inlet manifold.

The carburetor is one of the most important parts of a gasoline engine. A very simple device located near the inlet manifold, it mixes gasoline with air, providing a highly combustible fuel mixture to send into the cylinders. The throttle valve, located in the carburetor, is linked up to the accelerator pedal, and controls the engine speed by allowing more or less fuel to reach the cylinders.

The revolving cams, driven from the crankshaft, turn once for every two turns of the latter. One turn opens the inlet valve, the next opens the exhaust valve.

Inlet manifold

The descending piston sucks the mixture of fuel into the cylinder.

① Admission

The piston rises to compress the fuel tightly, raising its temperature greatly and so helping it to ignite.

A balancing counterweight helps the crankshaft to turn smoothly past the "dead points," when the piston connecting rod and crank are lined up straight.

② Compression (beginning)

The spark plug is timed to ignite once the piston has reached the top of its course, having tightly compressed the fuel. The explosion produced by the spark pushes the piston violently away again.

Burnt gases are expelled via the exhaust manifold, through mufflers, into the atmosphere.

③ Ignition

Exhaust manifold

④ Exhaust

The four-cycle gasoline engine is the type most commonly used for automobiles. During **admission** (1), the piston descends the cylinder, while the inlet valve is opened, and sucks in the mixture of fuel prepared by the carburetor. When the piston reaches the end of its course, the inlet valve closes. **Compression** (2) begins as the piston rises, pressing the fuel into a tight space near the spark plug, at the same time greatly raising the temperature. When the piston reaches the top of its course, an electric current is sent into the spark plug, which ignites the fuel. This is **ignition** (3). As the burning gas expands, it pushes the piston violently back and, through the connecting rod, gives the crankshaft a powerful turn. This moment is sometimes called the power stroke. As the piston returns the exhaust valve is opened, and the piston pushes the burnt gas out of the cylinder. When this **exhaust** (4) stroke is completed, another **admission** (1) stroke begins.

Here, simplified, are the principle parts of an engine, showing the relation of one part to another. Directly behind the flywheel lies the friction clutch, which engages the gears, and through which power is transmitted to the drive shaft, differential, and driving wheels.

Rocker arms

Valve spring

Inlet valve

Exhaust valve

Cylinder

Spark plug

Camshaft

Cam

Push rod

Piston rings: assure a tight fit between piston and cylinder

Piston pin

Connecting rod

Belt drive to fan

Chain drive to camshaft

"Big-end" bearing

Counterbalancing weights

Flywheel: its weighty spin assures the smoothness of the four cycles of the engine. Its perimeter is toothed in order to engage with the starter, to fire up the engine.

Anatomy of an Automobile

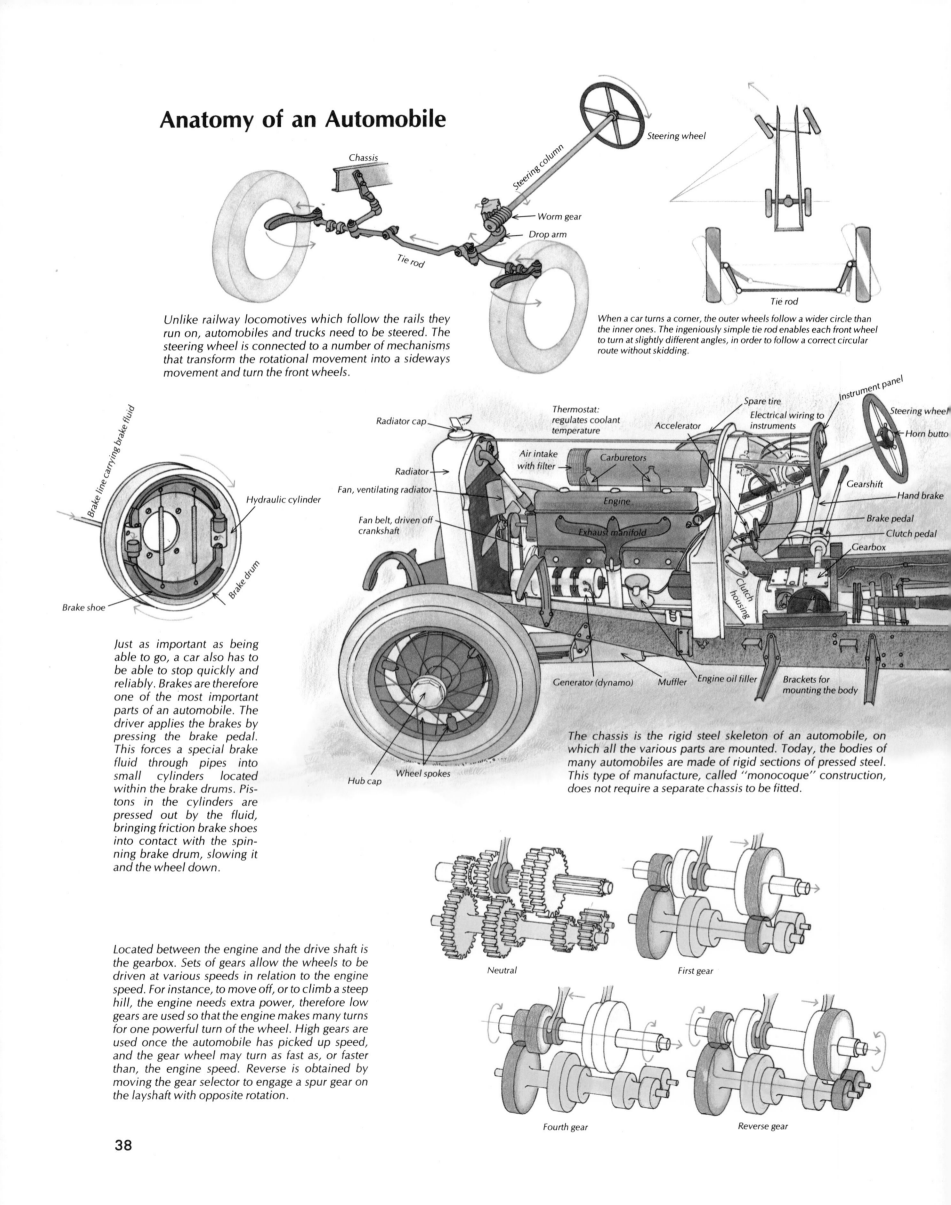

Chassis

Steering wheel

Steering column

Worm gear

Drop arm

Tie rod

Tie rod

Unlike railway locomotives which follow the rails they run on, automobiles and trucks need to be steered. The steering wheel is connected to a number of mechanisms that transform the rotational movement into a sideways movement and turn the front wheels.

When a car turns a corner, the outer wheels follow a wider circle than the inner ones. The ingeniously simple tie rod enables each front wheel to turn at slightly different angles, in order to follow a correct circular route without skidding.

Brake line carrying brake fluid

Hydraulic cylinder

Brake drum

Brake shoe

Brake drum

Radiator cap

Radiator

Fan, ventilating radiator

Fan belt, driven off crankshaft

Thermostat: regulates coolant temperature

Air intake with filter

Carburetors

Engine

Exhaust manifold

Spare tire

Accelerator

Electrical wiring to instruments

Instrument panel

Steering wheel

Horn butto

Gearshift

Hand brake

Brake pedal

Clutch pedal

Gearbox

Clutch housing

Generator (dynamo)

Muffler

Engine oil filler

Brackets for mounting the body

Hub cap

Wheel spokes

Just as important as being able to go, a car also has to be able to stop quickly and reliably. Brakes are therefore one of the most important parts of an automobile. The driver applies the brakes by pressing the brake pedal. This forces a special brake fluid through pipes into small cylinders located within the brake drums. Pistons in the cylinders are pressed out by the fluid, bringing friction brake shoes into contact with the spinning brake drum, slowing it and the wheel down.

The chassis is the rigid steel skeleton of an automobile, on which all the various parts are mounted. Today, the bodies of many automobiles are made of rigid sections of pressed steel. This type of manufacture, called "monocoque" construction, does not require a separate chassis to be fitted.

Located between the engine and the drive shaft is the gearbox. Sets of gears allow the wheels to be driven at various speeds in relation to the engine speed. For instance, to move off, or to climb a steep hill, the engine needs extra power, therefore low gears are used so that the engine makes many turns for one powerful turn of the wheel. High gears are used once the automobile has picked up speed, and the gear wheel may turn as fast as, or faster than, the engine speed. Reverse is obtained by moving the gear selector to engage a spur gear on the layshaft with opposite rotation.

Neutral

First gear

Fourth gear

Reverse gear

An automobile, like the human body, is made up of a great many different organs. The engine is its heart, bringing it to life, while the steering and brakes, like legs and feet, control its movements.

Although, over the years, external design has changed greatly, internally, cars today are still made up of the same basic organs. Let's take a closer look inside.

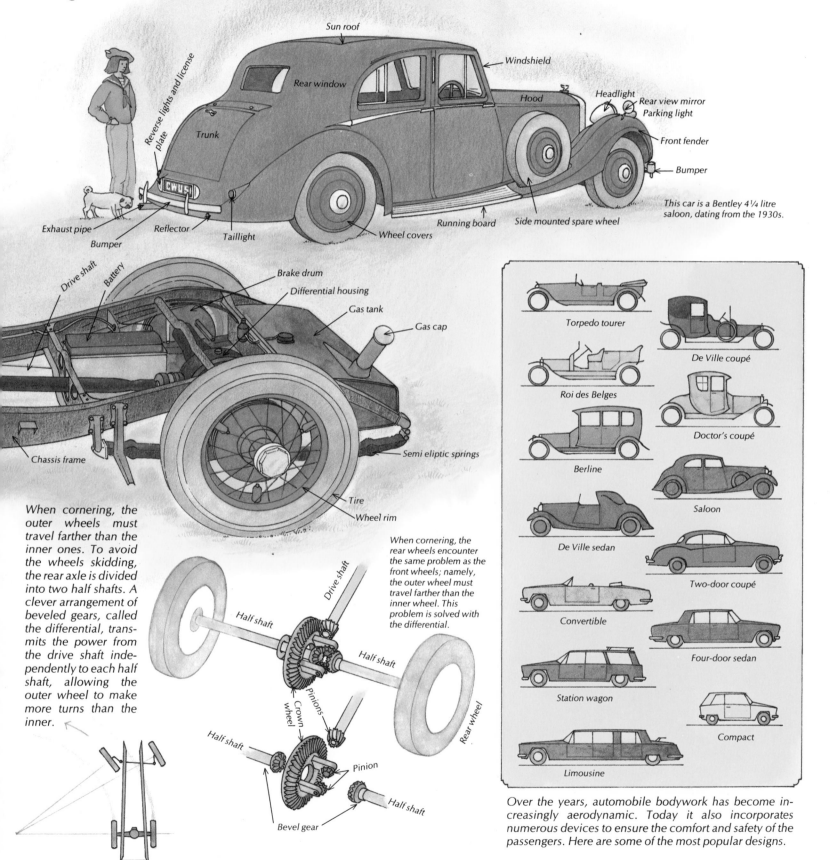

Sun roof

Windshield

Rear window

Hood

Headlight
Rear view mirror
Parking light

Reverse lights and license plate

Trunk

Front fender

Bumper

Exhaust pipe
Bumper
Reflector
Taillight
Wheel covers
Running board
Side mounted spare wheel

This car is a Bentley 4¼ litre saloon, dating from the 1930s.

Drive shaft
Battery
Brake drum
Differential housing
Gas tank
Gas cap

Chassis frame
Semi eliptic springs
Tire
Wheel rim

When cornering, the outer wheels must travel farther than the inner ones. To avoid the wheels skidding, the rear axle is divided into two half shafts. A clever arrangement of beveled gears, called the differential, transmits the power from the drive shaft independently to each half shaft, allowing the outer wheel to make more turns than the inner.

When cornering, the rear wheels encounter the same problem as the front wheels; namely, the outer wheel must travel farther than the inner wheel. This problem is solved with the differential.

Drive shaft
Half shaft
Half shaft
Pinions
Crown wheel
Half shaft
Pinion
Half shaft
Bevel gear
Rear wheel

Torpedo tourer
De Ville coupé
Roi des Belges
Doctor's coupé
Berline
Saloon
De Ville sedan
Two-door coupé
Convertible
Four-door sedan
Station wagon
Compact
Limousine

Over the years, automobile bodywork has become increasingly aerodynamic. Today it also incorporates numerous devices to ensure the comfort and safety of the passengers. Here are some of the most popular designs.

39

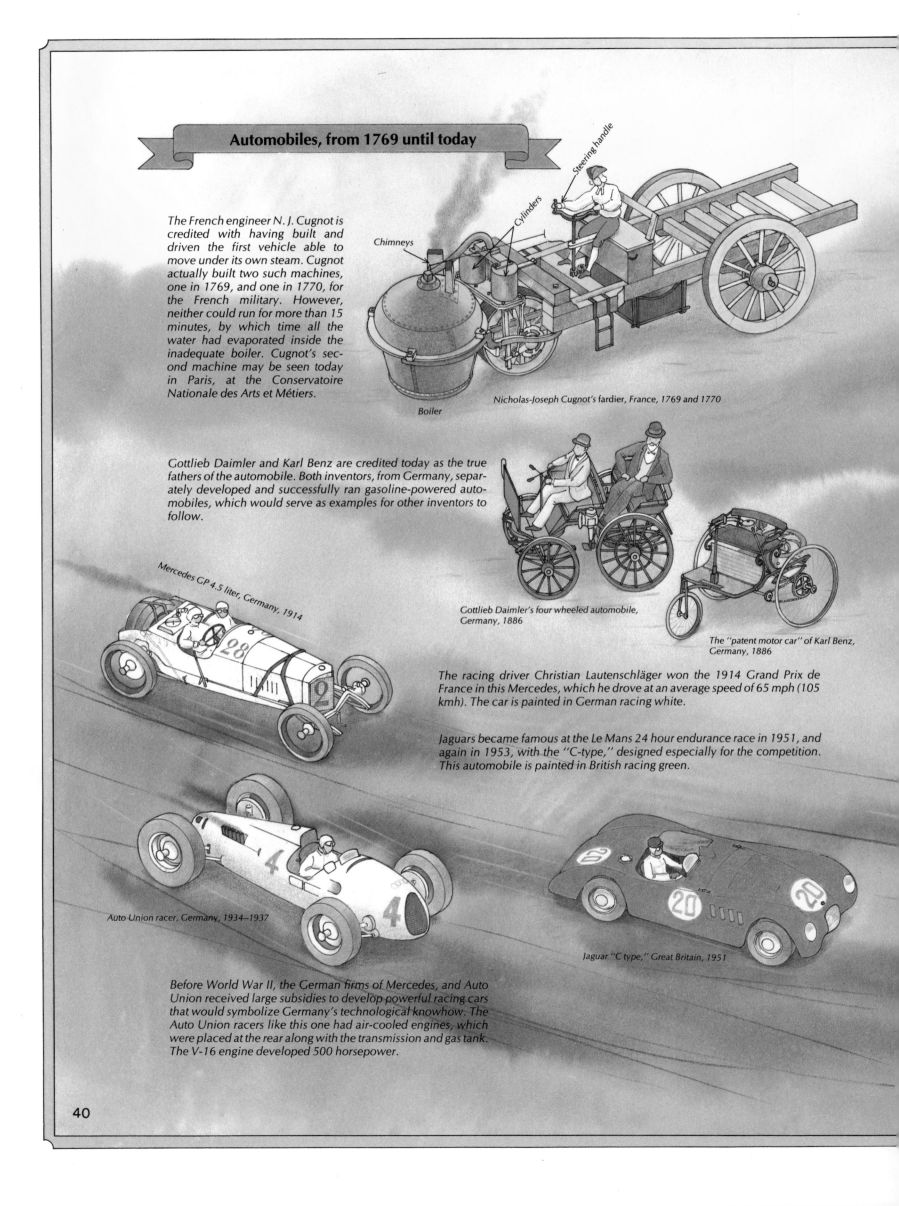

Automobiles, from 1769 until today

The French engineer N. J. Cugnot is credited with having built and driven the first vehicle able to move under its own steam. Cugnot actually built two such machines, one in 1769, and one in 1770, for the French military. However, neither could run for more than 15 minutes, by which time all the water had evaporated inside the inadequate boiler. Cugnot's second machine may be seen today in Paris, at the Conservatoire Nationale des Arts et Métiers.

Chimneys

Cylinders

Steering handle

Boiler

Nicholas-Joseph Cugnot's fardier, France, 1769 and 1770

Gottlieb Daimler and Karl Benz are credited today as the true fathers of the automobile. Both inventors, from Germany, separately developed and successfully ran gasoline-powered automobiles, which would serve as examples for other inventors to follow.

Gottlieb Daimler's four wheeled automobile, Germany, 1886

The "patent motor car" of Karl Benz, Germany, 1886

Mercedes GP 4.5 liter, Germany, 1914

The racing driver Christian Lautenschläger won the 1914 Grand Prix de France in this Mercedes, which he drove at an average speed of 65 mph (105 kmh). The car is painted in German racing white.

Jaguars became famous at the Le Mans 24 hour endurance race in 1951, and again in 1953, with the "C-type," designed especially for the competition. This automobile is painted in British racing green.

Auto Union racer, Germany, 1934–1937

Jaguar "C type," Great Britain, 1951

Before World War II, the German firms of Mercedes, and Auto Union received large subsidies to develop powerful racing cars that would symbolize Germany's technological knowhow. The Auto Union racers like this one had air-cooled engines, which were placed at the rear along with the transmission and gas tank. The V-16 engine developed 500 horsepower.

40

The inventor of the first railway locomotive, Richard Trevithick, also tested a road locomotive, in 1801. After driving several hundred yards, some mechanical trouble arose. Leaving the machine to celebrate with a meal at a nearby inn, Trevithick returned to find his machine had been completely burnt.

Steam carriage of William Henry James, Great Britain, 1828

Richard Trevithick's ''Camborne'' road locomotive, Great Britain, 1801

Perhaps the most famous automobile of all is the Ford Model T, manufactured from 1908 to 1927. About 15 million of these sturdy, inexpensive vehicles were made. By 1926, you could buy one new for only $290. Half the automobiles you met on the road were Model Ts.

In the early 1800s, several steam carriages were designed in Britain. However, the Locomotive Act of 1831 required all mechanized vehicles to be preceded by a man on foot, waving a red flag!

In 1934, Citroën built a revolutionary automobile, which remained in production until 1957. It had front wheel drive, a new gear system, hydraulic brakes, and a monocoque body.

Citroën 7S ''Traction Avant,'' France, 1934

Ford Model T, USA, this one dating from 1922

Starter handle

Rear mounted, air-cooled engine

Folding canvas top

Just before the outbreak of World War II, the German government commissioned Ferdinand Porsche to design an inexpensive ''people's car.'' The resulting ''Volkswagen,'' nicknamed ''Beetle,'' went on to be manufactured in millions.

Volkswagen ''Beetle,'' 1953 model, Germany

Windshield

Ford GT ''Mark II,'' USA, 1966

During World War II, the US Army asked American automobile manufacturers to design a lightweight, four-wheel drive ''general purpose'' truck. The resulting ''GP'' truck soon became known as the ''Jeep.''

''Jeep,'' USA, World War II

Winch

The Ford Motor Company swept up the first three places in the 1966 Le Mans endurance race with a trio of ''GTs.'' Experience gained in racing competitions permits manufacturers to improve the performance, durability, and safety of their standard production cars.

Formula I races are the most important Grand Prix races today. Formula I racers are single seaters and their engine size and body design are subject to special racing rules.

Ferrari Formula I racer, Italy, 1963

Trucks and buses from 1916 until today

Foden "six wheeler" steam tractor, Great Britain, 1916

Before the arrival of powerful diesel-engined trucks in the 1920s, steam-powered tractors were widely used for any heavy tasks, whether they were for transporting, for road building, or for use on the farm.

Ticket conductor

Parisian omnibuses were famed for their open platform at the rear, where one entered the bus and from which one could get a good view of the city while en route. The Schneider "H" buses drove through the streets of Paris between the two World Wars.

Open platform

Refrigerator trucks ensure that any perishables, whether they be meat, fish, fruit, vegetables, or dairy products, are brought from the producer to the stores without any spoilage.

Schneider "Type H" omnibus, France, 1916

Refrigerator unit

co-op

Saurer "D 290," Switzerland

Land Rover, Great Britain

Trucks powered on all four wheels are known as having four-wheel drive. Such vehicles, with their exceptional grip, are handy for reaching places that would normally be inaccessible. The Land Rover, popular worldwide, can be adapted for the most varied tasks.

International Harvester "Transtar 4300," USA

Big tractor-trailers like this one are a common sight on American highways, where trucks have replaced the railways for much freight traffic.

Trucks and buses do a variety of different tasks, so there are many different types. Here are some common ones.

Van

Tank truck

Tractor-trailer

Pickup truck

Flatbed truck and container

Minibus

Dump truck

Camper

In the United States where children often live miles from school, bright yellow buses carry them to and from home. At bus stops, while school children board or get off, red flashing lights on the roof command other vehicles to halt, allowing the children to cross the street in safety.

Flashing red lights

Wayne-bodied schoolbus, USA

DRINKA PINTA MILKA DAY

London Transport "Routemaster" omnibus, Great Britain, 1950s

One way to carry more people in a bus is to add an extra floor! Double-decker buses are a continuation of earlier horsedrawn omnibuses which had an open-air "imperial" upper deck for passengers. Although many cities have done away with their double-deckers, the London buses have become world famous. A window seat up top is a fine place to see the city!

This modern tractor-trailer is a car transporter. The upper decks can be lowered and small ramps extended to allow vehicles to be driven on and off the truck. Transporters are used mainly to deliver new automobiles from the factory to dealers.

Renault "GB 231," France

43

A Roman road

The ancient Romans are famous for the fine roads they built, which linked the major cities of their empire. While rendering travel and the trade of goods much easier, the roads also provided unhindered routes for their legions of soldiers, who might be called to any corner of the empire in case of unrest.

Ancient Roman roads were always built as straight as possible. Here, surveyors line-up road markers, sighting through the plumb lines of a "groma." A level with a shallow trough for water, known as a chorobates, checks that the road has no sags or bumps!

Birota: two-wheeled cart

Chorobates: water level

Marker

Marker

Basalt rock slabs

Groma: surveying instrument

Surveyor sighting markers

Bridge of wood and stone

Small stones

Basalt slabs

Cement

Milestone

Mixing mortar cement

Crushing stones to make gravel

The Open Road

Most land vehicles need a good, hard-wearing surface to drive on. Although railroad design has not changed too much since Stephenson's *Rocket* puffed along the Liverpool and Manchester Railway, roads have developed remarkably to carry the ever increasing number of vehicles of all shapes and sizes that constantly drive over them.

Good, well-built roads, even the one outside your door, have made traveling today as comfortable and natural as breathing.

Although good highways have made automobile travel a pleasure, they have also, in many places, become a pest. In most cities today, cars are used so much that even the widest highways are always congested.

With so much international road traffic today, the governments of many nations have agreed to use a standardized international road sign system. Wherever he may be, even if he doesn't understand the words, a driver will always know the rules of the road simply by following the symbols.

SPEED LIMIT 55 — *Speed Limit*

Right Curve Ahead

DO NOT ENTER — *Do Not Enter*

YIELD — *Yield*

STOP — *Stop*

No Parking

R X R — *Railroad Crossing*

Two Way Traffic

DETOUR — *Detour*

After the fall of the Roman Empire, through much of history, road building was carried out in piecemeal fashion with unskilled laborers. For a time in France, every male citizen was required to spend some of his time repairing local roads.

A well built road in the 18th century

Level and sights

Milestone

Quadrant

Tamping tool

Fine gravel

Coarse gravel

Large, upright stones

Well drained roadway with a raise in the middle.

It was only in the 18th century that an applied science of road building took shape. Thanks to the initiative of Pierre-Marie-Jérome Tresaguet in France and to John Loudon McAdam and Thomas Telford, both from Scotland, roads began to be built with care for good drainage, gentle gradients and a firm surface.

Automobiles brought about a radical change in the construction of roads, which from 1905 were covered by a layer of coal tar. As both the number and the speed of automobiles increased, it became necessary to provide them with big, wide highways to drive on. In Italy, in 1925, the first "autostrada" was built between Milan and Varese. Today, networks of highways link major cities all over the world, facilitating trade and travel.

A modern highway

Exit lane

"Flyover" bridge

Entry lane

Emergency telephone

Curb

Automobile associations provide breakdown service.

Curb markers

Driving lane

Hot asphalt

Roller

Overtaking lane

Paver

Dump truck

Metal crash fence

Center meridian

Road works

Exit lane

Things that
Sail

Earth's Natural Highway

Although almost everyone on Earth lives on dry land, most of our planet's surface is covered by water. Seen from space, the Earth looks blue, which is why it is sometimes called the Blue Planet.

A sailor from any port on Earth can reach any other port, anywhere in the world, by sailing across the sea, Earth's natural highway.

Roads and railways crisscross the world, but they are a very modern means of travel and transport. A couple of hundred years ago there were no railways, and the roads were often no more than bumpy, muddy tracks. For hundreds of years the best way to travel was by water. This is why most of the world's large cities are at the edge of the sea or on the banks of a great river.

The civilization which grew up in ancient Egypt, three and a half thousand years ago, depended on the Nile River. Around the towns, the temples, the pyramids and the fields, lay desert. The river was the highway which linked the towns together. Other ancient civilizations grew up on the banks of the Tigris and the Euphrates in Asia, the Indus and the Ganges in India, and the Yellow River in China.

Three thousand years later, when men set out from Europe to search for new lands across the sea, they went by ship. They explored the great continents of Africa, Asia, North and South America and, eventually, Australia, by sailing up the rivers that led into the unknown lands.

Thousands of years ago, when people first began to build settlements to live in, boats and ships were the best and safest way of traveling from place to place, and the rivers and the sea were their natural highways.

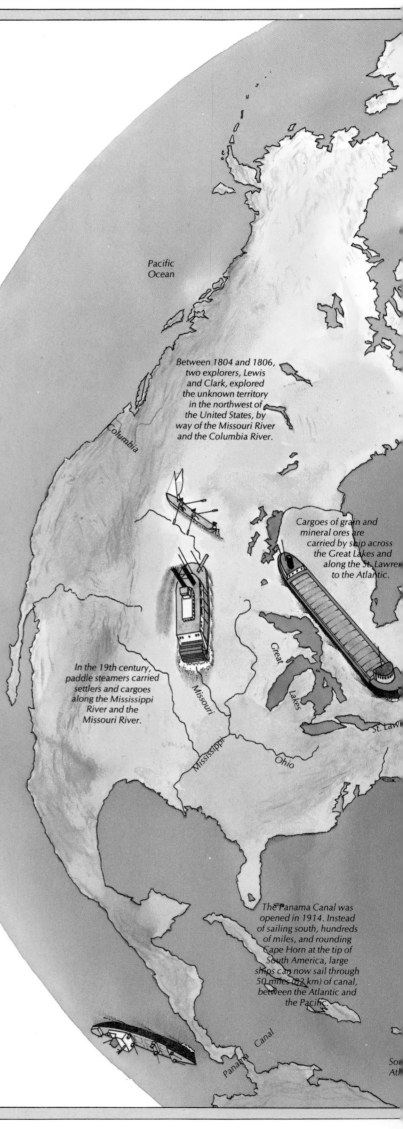

Pacific Ocean

Between 1804 and 1806, two explorers, Lewis and Clark, explored the unknown territory in the northwest of the United States, by way of the Missouri River and the Columbia River.

Columbia

Cargoes of grain and mineral ores are carried by ship across the Great Lakes and along the St. Lawrence to the Atlantic.

In the 19th century, paddle steamers carried settlers and cargoes along the Mississippi River and the Missouri River.

Great Lakes

Missouri

Mississippi

Ohio

St. Lawrence

The Panama Canal was opened in 1914. Instead of sailing south, hundreds of miles, and rounding Cape Horn at the tip of South America, large ships can now sail through 50 miles (82 km) of canal, between the Atlantic and the Pacific.

Panama Canal

South Atlantic

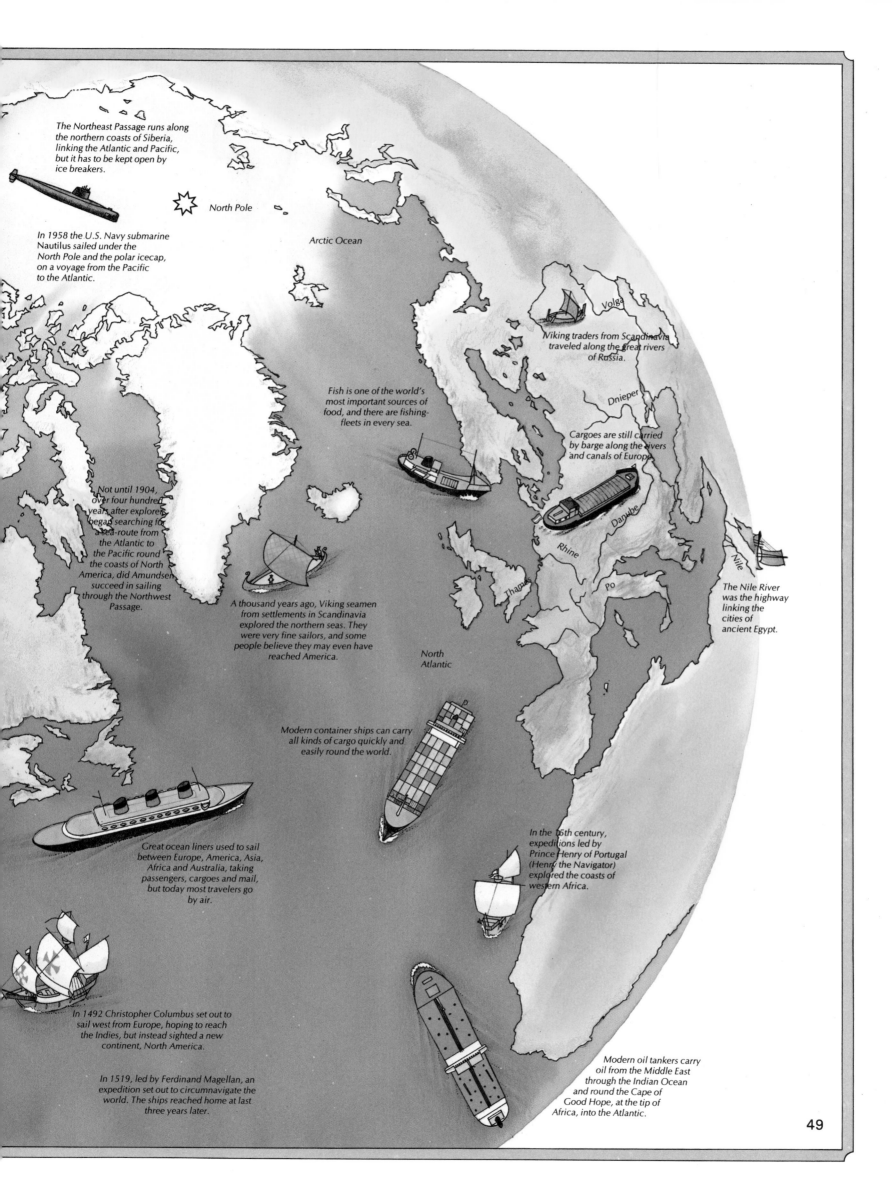

The Northeast Passage runs along the northern coasts of Siberia, linking the Atlantic and Pacific, but it has to be kept open by ice breakers.

In 1958 the U.S. Navy submarine Nautilus sailed under the North Pole and the polar icecap, on a voyage from the Pacific to the Atlantic.

North Pole

Arctic Ocean

Viking traders from Scandinavia traveled along the great rivers of Russia.

Volga

Dnieper

Fish is one of the world's most important sources of food, and there are fishing-fleets in every sea.

Cargoes are still carried by barge along the rivers and canals of Europe.

Not until 1904, over four hundred years after explorers began searching for a sea-route from the Atlantic to the Pacific round the coasts of North America, did Amundsen succeed in sailing through the Northwest Passage.

Danube

Rhine

Po

Nile

Thames

A thousand years ago, Viking seamen from settlements in Scandinavia explored the northern seas. They were very fine sailors, and some people believe they may even have reached America.

North Atlantic

The Nile River was the highway linking the cities of ancient Egypt.

Modern container ships can carry all kinds of cargo quickly and easily round the world.

Great ocean liners used to sail between Europe, America, Asia, Africa and Australia, taking passengers, cargoes and mail, but today most travelers go by air.

In the 15th century, expeditions led by Prince Henry of Portugal (Henry the Navigator) explored the coasts of western Africa.

In 1492 Christopher Columbus set out to sail west from Europe, hoping to reach the Indies, but instead sighted a new continent, North America.

In 1519, led by Ferdinand Magellan, an expedition set out to circumnavigate the world. The ships reached home at last three years later.

Modern oil tankers carry oil from the Middle East through the Indian Ocean and round the Cape of Good Hope, at the tip of Africa, into the Atlantic.

49

More than two thousand years ago, a Greek scientist called Archimedes made a discovery. He was trying to think of a way of checking whether a crown made for the king was pure gold, or gold mixed with a cheaper metal. He stepped into a bath tub full of water, and the tub overflowed. Archimedes jumped out of the tub and ran through the streets shouting, "Eureka! Eureka", which means "I have found it! I have found it!" What had he found?

Ευρηχα

"Eureka!"

Archimedes' Principle

When an object is immersed in water, it pushes aside, or displaces, enough water to make room for itself, and the volume of displaced water equals the volume of the object. If you weigh the object, and then immerse it in water and weigh it again, it loses weight, and the weight it loses equals the weight of water it displaces.

Archimedes immersed the crown, to discover what volume of metal it contained. He then immersed a lump of gold weighing the same as the crown, and it displaced a different volume of water. The crown was not pure gold.

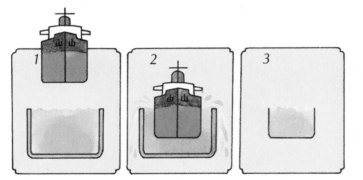

(1) Consider the case of a ship.
(2) The ship displaces water.
(3) The volume of water displaced equals the volume of the part of the ship that is immersed.

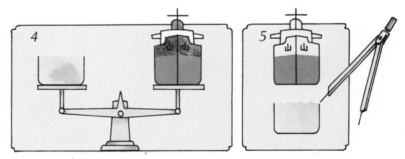

(4) The weight of water displaced equals the weight of the part of the ship below the waterline.
(5) Because the total volume of the ship is greater than the volume of water displaced, it floats.

To test Archimedes' Principle, take a paper cup, a measuring cup, and a precise weighing machine, such as a scale.

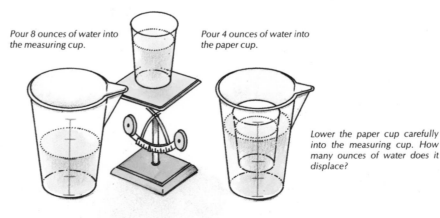

Pour 8 ounces of water into the measuring cup.

Pour 4 ounces of water into the paper cup.

Lower the paper cup carefully into the measuring cup. How many ounces of water does it displace?

If you immerse a lump of metal in water, the volume of water it displaces equals its own volume; but the lump of metal weighs more than the water, so it sinks.

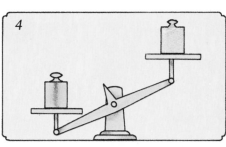

If, however, you hammer the lump of metal into a dish shape, it will float, and the water it displaces will weigh more than it does.

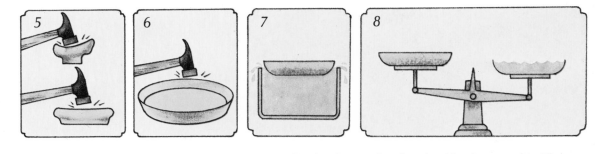

The weight and volume of a ship are measured in tonnage. Displacement tonnage is the total weight of a ship and everything on board; gross register tonnage, the ship's capacity; deadweight tonnage, the weight of the cargo, stores and fuel; net register tonnage, the ship's capacity for carrying cargo and passengers.

Loading levels are painted on the side of a cargo ship. There are different levels for different climates and seasons. When the ship is fully loaded, the appropriate mark should be at or above water level. Samuel Plimsoll brought in the first such line, the Plimsoll Mark, in 1876, to protect the lives of seamen.

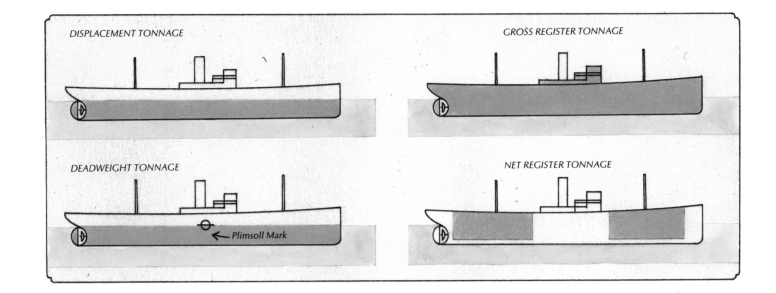

DISPLACEMENT TONNAGE

GROSS REGISTER TONNAGE

DEADWEIGHT TONNAGE

← Plimsoll Mark

NET REGISTER TONNAGE

The lines on the left are the loading lines for wooden ships.

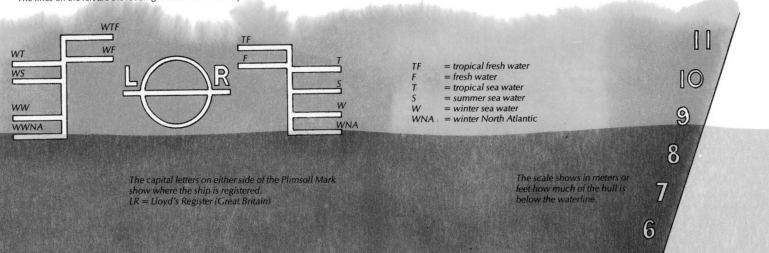

WTF
WT   WF
WS
WW
WWNA

TF
F
T
S
W
WNA

TF = tropical fresh water
F = fresh water
T = tropical sea water
S = summer sea water
W = winter sea water
WNA = winter North Atlantic

LR

11
10
9
8
7
6

The capital letters on either side of the Plimsoll Mark show where the ship is registered.
LR = Lloyd's Register (Great Britain)

The scale shows in meters or feet how much of the hull is below the waterline.

Water Sleds

Boats and ships don't run on wheels. A boat slides through the water on its hull, rather like someone tobogganing down a slope.

Mast

Cabin

Movable hatches cover the hold.

It is easy to punt a boat through shallow water by pushing the long punt poles against the riverbed.

52

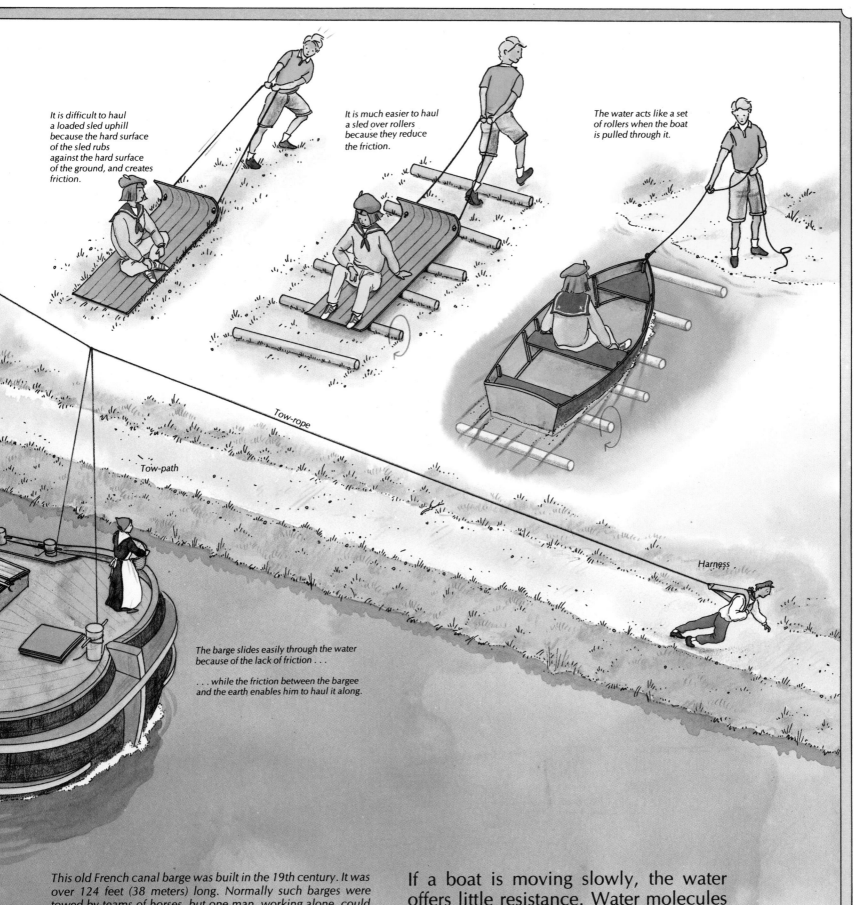

It is difficult to haul a loaded sled uphill because the hard surface of the sled rubs against the hard surface of the ground, and creates friction.

It is much easier to haul a sled over rollers because they reduce the friction.

The water acts like a set of rollers when the boat is pulled through it.

Tow-rope

Tow-path

Harness

The barge slides easily through the water because of the lack of friction . . .

. . . while the friction between the bargee and the earth enables him to haul it along.

This old French canal barge was built in the 19th century. It was over 124 feet (38 meters) long. Normally such barges were towed by teams of horses, but one man, working alone, could tow the barge if need be, though when fully loaded it weighed over 280 tons.

If a boat is moving slowly, the water offers little resistance. Water molecules glide easily over one another, and a boat slides over them almost effortlessly. And as a boat displaces its own weight when it floats on water, one man, working alone, can haul a barge carrying a load of several hundred tons.

Oars and Sails

When a boat is on the open water, it has to be propelled forward, or it will drift helplessly. One of the simplest ways of doing this is to row, using oars.

An oar is a lever. By exerting strength at one end of a lever, you can move a much greater weight, or overcome a much greater resistance, than you could deal with on your own. A rower uses the oars as a pair of levers, and drives the boat forward, stroke by stroke.

The mast is lowered, and the sail stowed on deck, when not in use.

In ancient times, galley slaves had to row ships in the Mediterranean Sea. It was hard, inhuman work. Sometimes, if they were lucky and the wind was blowing in the right direction, a sail could be hoisted so that the wind's strength drove the ship along, but any change of direction brought the oars out again.

These two ships were built in ancient Egypt, during the reign of Sahure (2540–2421 B.C.). The eye painted on the ship's prow is to help her "see" the way. The thick cord running from the prow to the stern, over the crutches, helped to strengthen the hull in high seas which could have broken her back.

54

Direction of the wind

The ship is steered by using the upright oars at the stern.

When a fresh breeze blows from the stern, it pushes the boat forward through the water.

Wings and Sails

Air passing over the upper surface of the airplane's wing has to travel faster because of the curved shape. This means that the air particles are spread out more thinly, and the pressure is less. The air below the wing is moving more slowly, over a shorter distance, so its pressure is greater.

Lift

Airfoil

Faster air

Direction of flight

Lift

Slower air

Airfoil

Airfoil

Faster air

Airfoil

Slower air

A bird's wing, the wings of an airplane, and the sail on a sailboat, are similar in shape. They are all airfoils. The upper, or outer, surface is curved. This means that the air particles must travel faster across it, so that they are spread more thinly. There is less air pressure on the upper surface of the wing, or the outer surface of the sail, than there is on the lower or inner surface. The higher pressure below the wing lifts the bird or airplane into the air, and the higher pressure on the concave side of the sail drives the boat through the water.

Imagine a pair of sails laid flat, like wings. As they fill with wind, they take on the same curved shape as the wings of an airplane. The sail is filled by a cushion of wind and acts like the other airfoils.

3

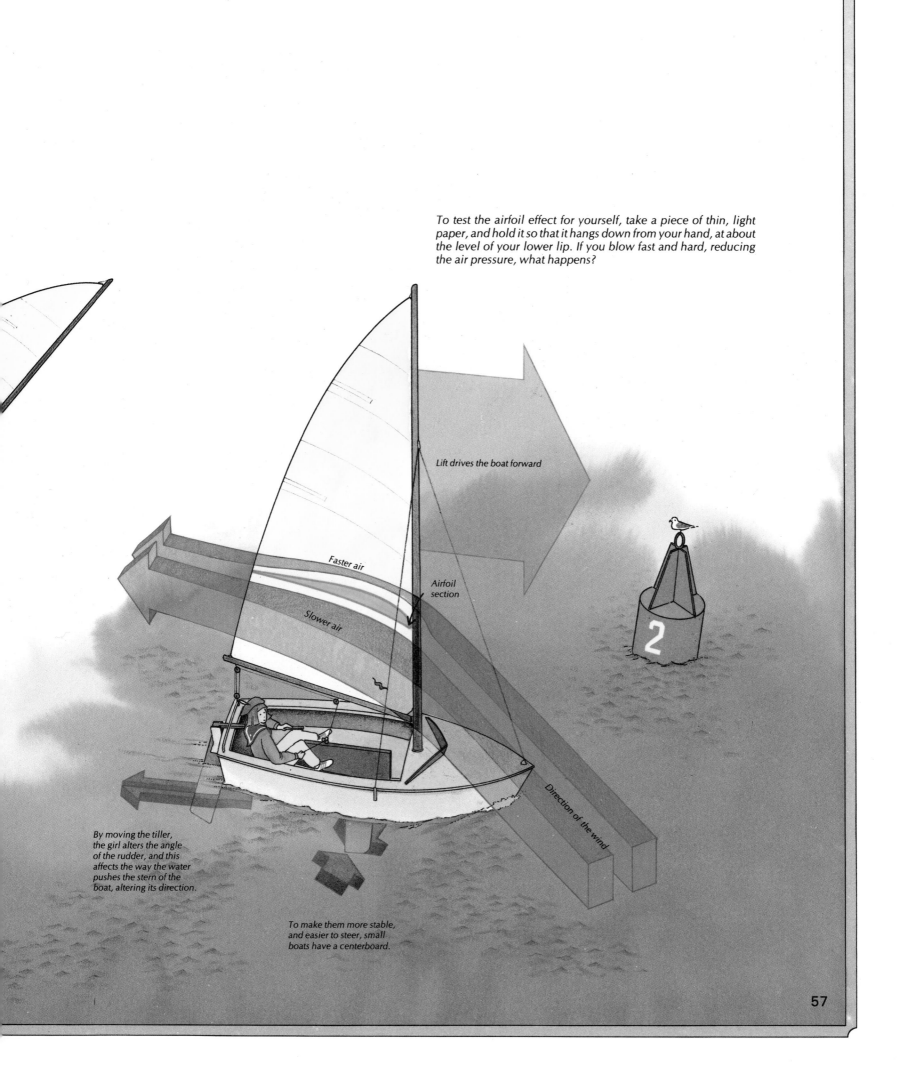

To test the airfoil effect for yourself, take a piece of thin, light paper, and hold it so that it hangs down from your hand, at about the level of your lower lip. If you blow fast and hard, reducing the air pressure, what happens?

Lift drives the boat forward

Faster air

Airfoil section

Slower air

Direction of the wind

By moving the tiller, the girl alters the angle of the rudder, and this affects the way the water pushes the stern of the boat, altering its direction.

To make them more stable, and easier to steer, small boats have a centerboard.

2

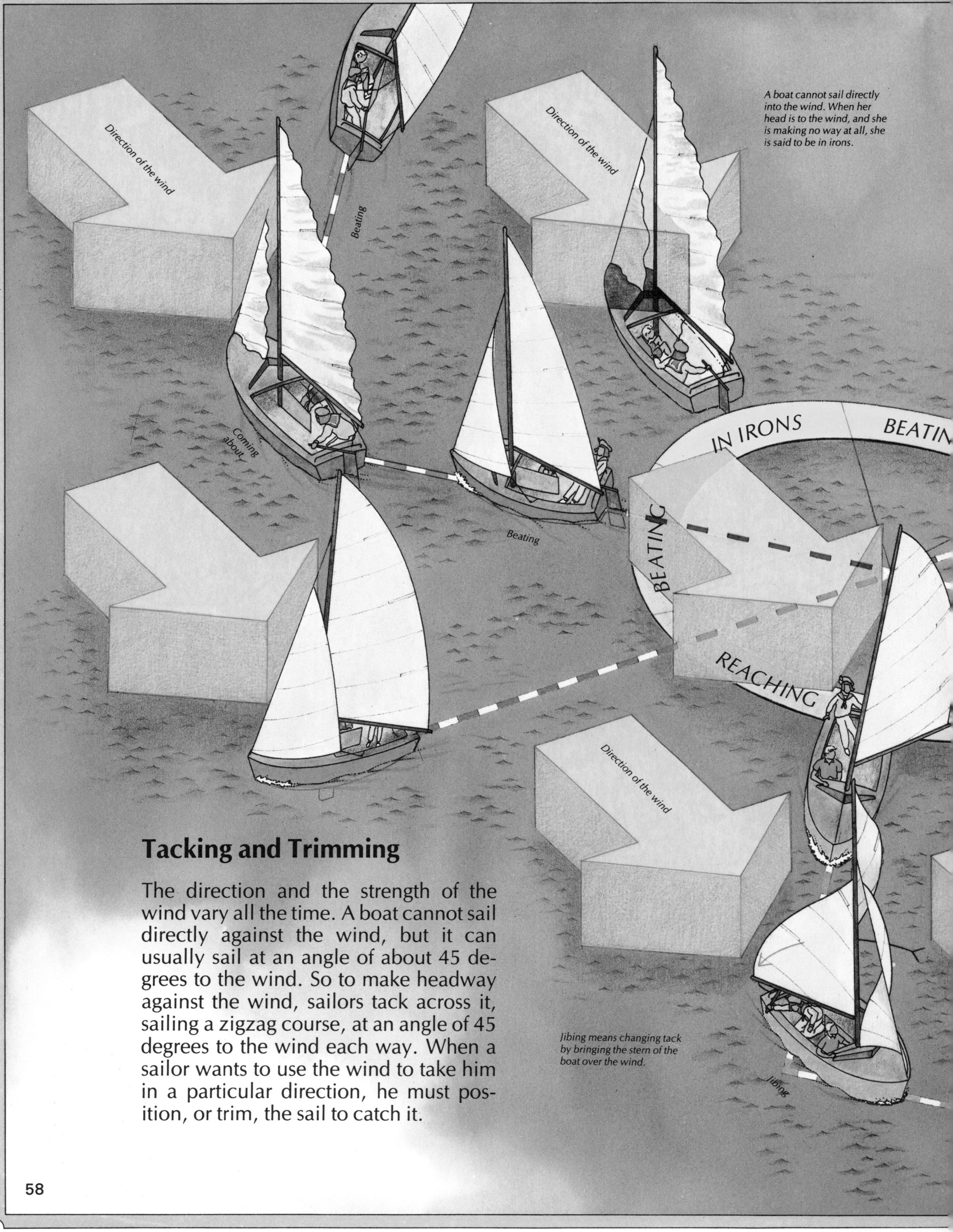

Direction of the wind

Beating

Direction of the wind

A boat cannot sail directly into the wind. When her head is to the wind, and she is making no way at all, she is said to be in irons.

Coming about

Beating

IN IRONS

BEATIN

BEATING

REACHING

Direction of the wind

Tacking and Trimming

The direction and the strength of the wind vary all the time. A boat cannot sail directly against the wind, but it can usually sail at an angle of about 45 degrees to the wind. So to make headway against the wind, sailors tack across it, sailing a zigzag course, at an angle of 45 degrees to the wind each way. When a sailor wants to use the wind to take him in a particular direction, he must position, or trim, the sail to catch it.

Jibing means changing tack by bringing the stern of the boat over the wind.

Jibing

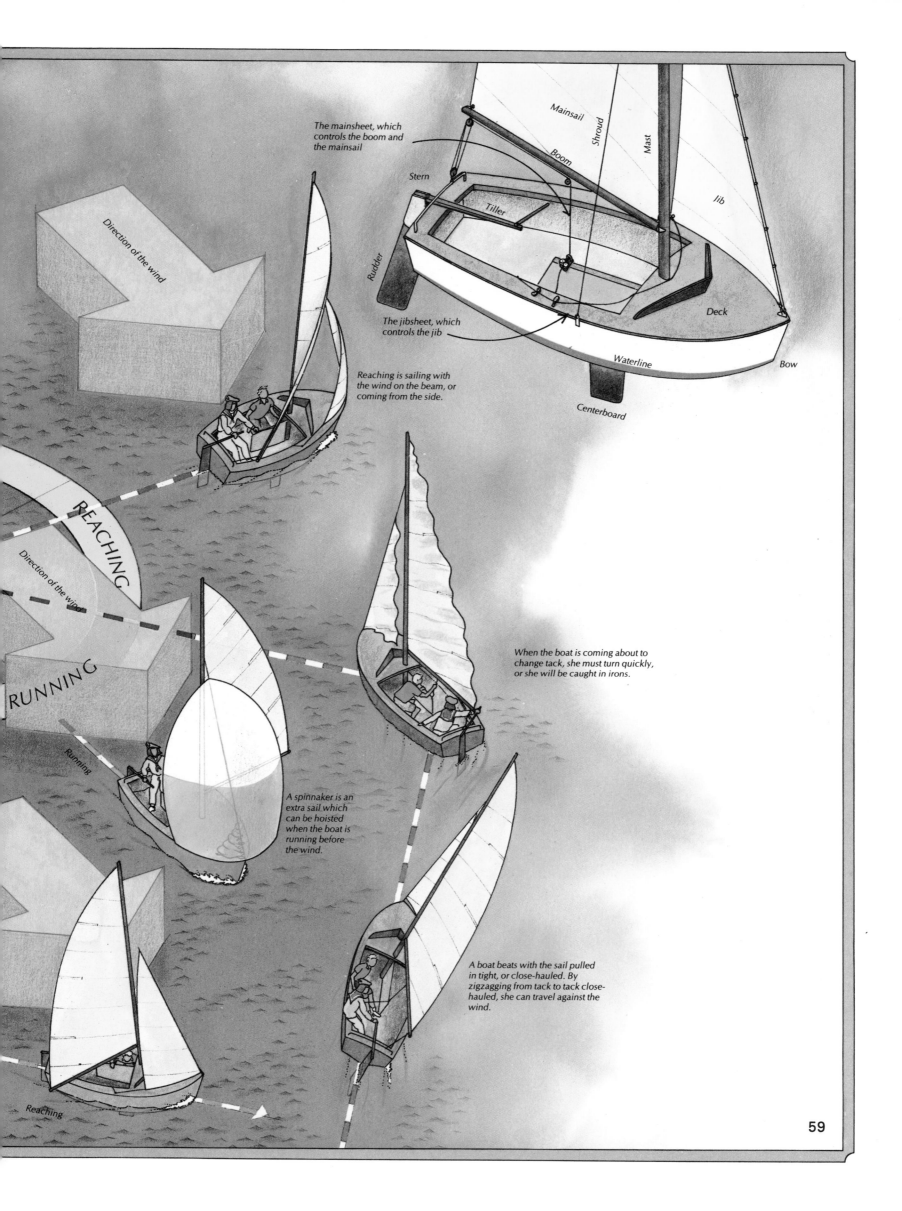

The mainsheet, which controls the boom and the mainsail

Mainsail

Shroud

Mast

Boom

Stern

Tiller

Jib

Rudder

Deck

The jibsheet, which controls the jib

Waterline

Bow

Reaching is sailing with the wind on the beam, or coming from the side.

Centerboard

Direction of the wind

REACHING

Direction of the wind

RUNNING

Running

A spinnaker is an extra sail which can be hoisted when the boat is running before the wind.

When the boat is coming about to change tack, she must turn quickly, or she will be caught in irons.

A boat beats with the sail pulled in tight, or close-hauled. By zigzagging from tack to tack close-hauled, she can travel against the wind.

Reaching

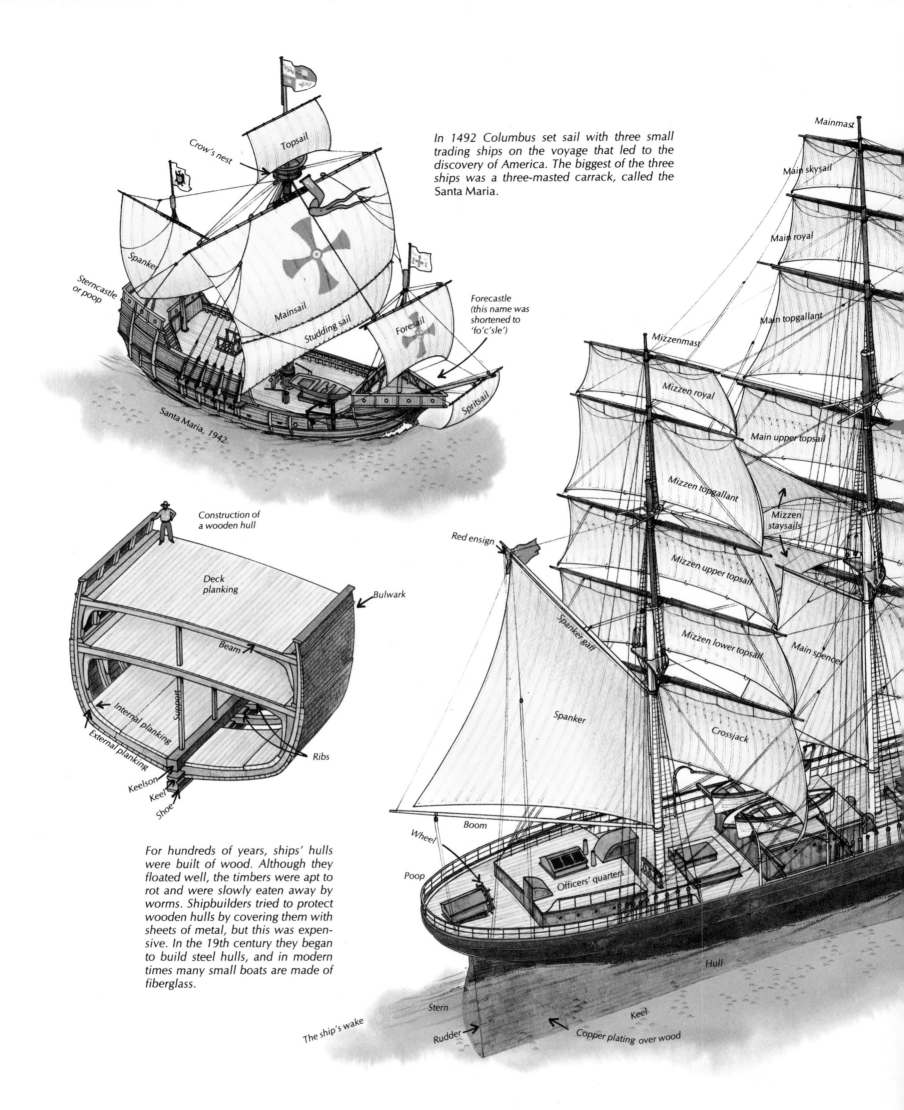

In 1492 Columbus set sail with three small trading ships on the voyage that led to the discovery of America. The biggest of the three ships was a three-masted carrack, called the Santa Maria.

Crow's nest
Topsail
Spanker
Sterncastle or poop
Mainsail
Studding sail
Foresail
Forecastle (this name was shortened to 'fo'c'sle')
Spritsail
Santa Maria, 1942

Construction of a wooden hull

Deck planking
Bulwark
Beam
Internal planking
External planking
Support
Ribs
Keelson
Keel
Shoe

For hundreds of years, ships' hulls were built of wood. Although they floated well, the timbers were apt to rot and were slowly eaten away by worms. Shipbuilders tried to protect wooden hulls by covering them with sheets of metal, but this was expensive. In the 19th century they began to build steel hulls, and in modern times many small boats are made of fiberglass.

Mainmast
Main skysail
Main royal
Main topgallant
Mizzenmast
Mizzen royal
Main upper topsail
Mizzen topgallant
Mizzen staysails
Mizzen upper topsail
Red ensign
Spanker gaff
Mizzen lower topsail
Main spencer
Spanker
Crossjack
Boom
Wheel
Poop
Officers' quarters
Hull
Stern
Keel
The ship's wake
Rudder
Copper plating over wood

Sailing Ships

On a sailing ship, every sail, every rope, every piece of equipment, has its own name. The three ships shown on these pages are drawn to about the same scale. They cover 450 years of the history of sail: the *Santa Maria* from the days when men were setting out on long, dangerous voyages in search of new sea-routes and new lands; the *Cutty Sark* from the time when a swift passage was the thing that mattered most and every inch of canvas counted; and the *Rainbow*, a fast and elegant racing yacht.

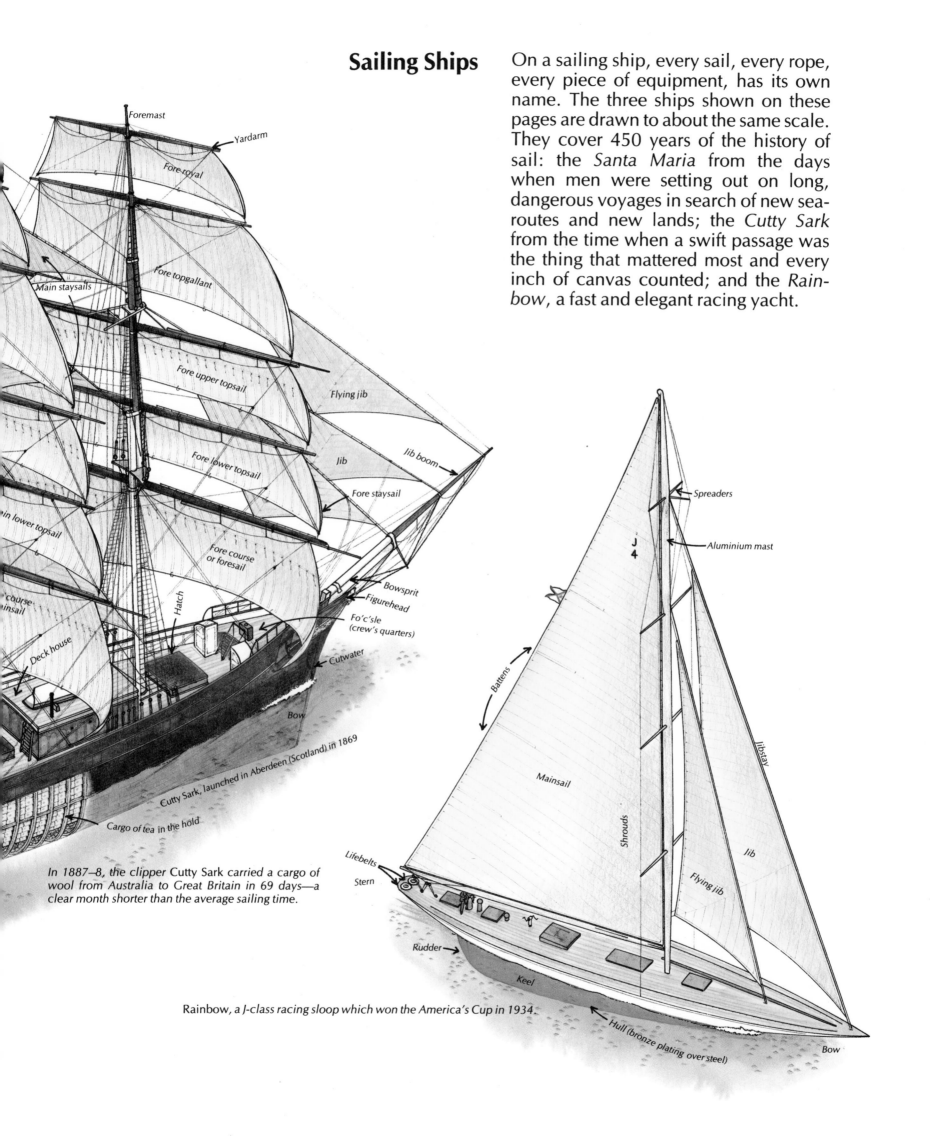

Foremast

Yardarm

Fore royal

Main staysails

Fore topgallant

Fore upper topsail

Flying jib

Fore lower topsail

Jib

Jib boom

Fore staysail

in lower topsail

Fore course
or foresail

Bowsprit

Figurehead

Fo'c'sle
(crew's quarters)

course
insail

Hatch

Cutwater

Deck house

Bow

Cargo of tea in the hold

Cutty Sark, launched in Aberdeen (Scotland) in 1869

In 1887–8, the clipper Cutty Sark carried a cargo of wool from Australia to Great Britain in 69 days—a clear month shorter than the average sailing time.

Spreaders

Aluminium mast

J
4

Jibstay

Battens

Mainsail

Shrouds

Jib

Flying jib

Lifebelts

Stern

Rudder

Keel

Hull (bronze plating over steel)

Bow

Rainbow, a J-class racing sloop which won the America's Cup in 1934.

Some Sailing Ships

Trading ships like this one sailed the North Sea in the 13th and 14th centuries. In place of the steering oar there was now a rudder, hinged to the sternpost of the ship.

Trading ship, 13th century

Viking longship about AD 1000

The Vikings' steer-board, or steering oar, gave us the word starboard which is still used for the right-hand side of a ship. The left-hand is the port side.

This 12-meter racer competed for the America's Cup, the most famous yachting trophy of our day.

Weatherly, USA, 1962

The 19th century clipper ships carried cargo and passengers at a fast clip—bringing tea and spices from the Orient and wool from Australia, and taking prospectors to join the Gold Rush in California.

Republic, USA, 1800

The Mayflower crossed the Atlantic in 66 days, carrying the Pilgrim Fathers to found their first settlement in America.

Chinese junk, about 1900

Oriental junks have sailed the coasts and seas of eastern Asia for centuries. Their paneled sails are stiffened with slats of bamboo.

Mayflower, England, 1620

Elsie, USA, 1910

S-class, USA

Today, most people who go sailing choose small sailboats. Sailing has become a sport. These small, lively, pleasure craft are sailed for fun.

Thistle, USA

Schooners were developed in America in the 19th century. Elsie was a fishing vessel and fished the Grand Banks off Newfoundland.

Paddles

The paddles which canoeists use are similar in shape to the duck's feet.

A duck uses its webbed feet to paddle its way through the water.

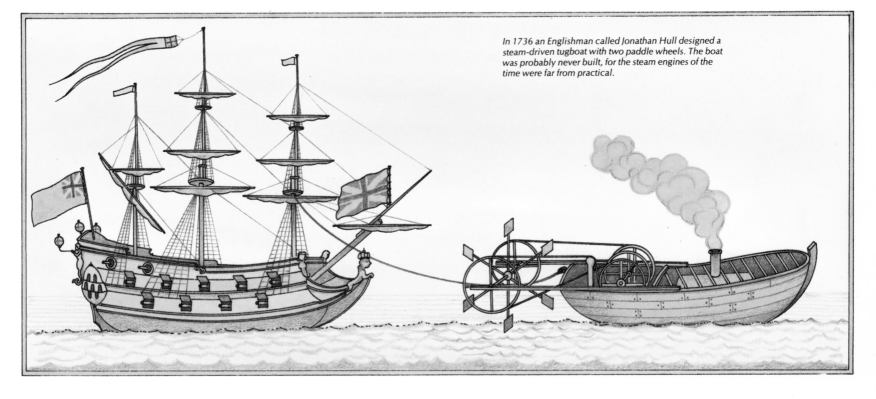

In 1736 an Englishman called Jonathan Hull designed a steam-driven tugboat with two paddle wheels. The boat was probably never built, for the steam engines of the time were far from practical.

Sailing ships depend entirely on the wind, but its direction and force vary all the time. If it begins to blow dangerously hard, so that it may rip the sails, snap the rigging and even break the mast, the sailors must shorten sail by reefing, or take down the sails altogether. If the wind drops, on the other hand, the ship may be becalmed.

For centuries, water mills have harnessed the force of rushing water by using it to turn a water wheel which is linked to the millstones. The invention of the steam engine led to experiments with steam-driven paddle wheels, as a way of driving ships along.

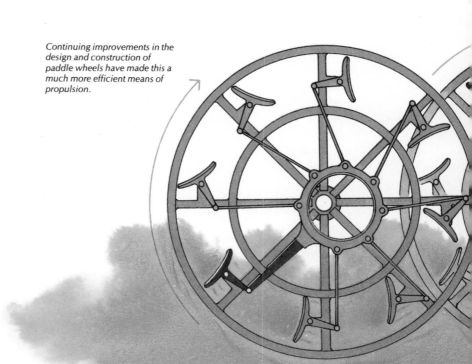

Continuing improvements in the design and construction of paddle wheels have made this a much more efficient means of propulsion.

64

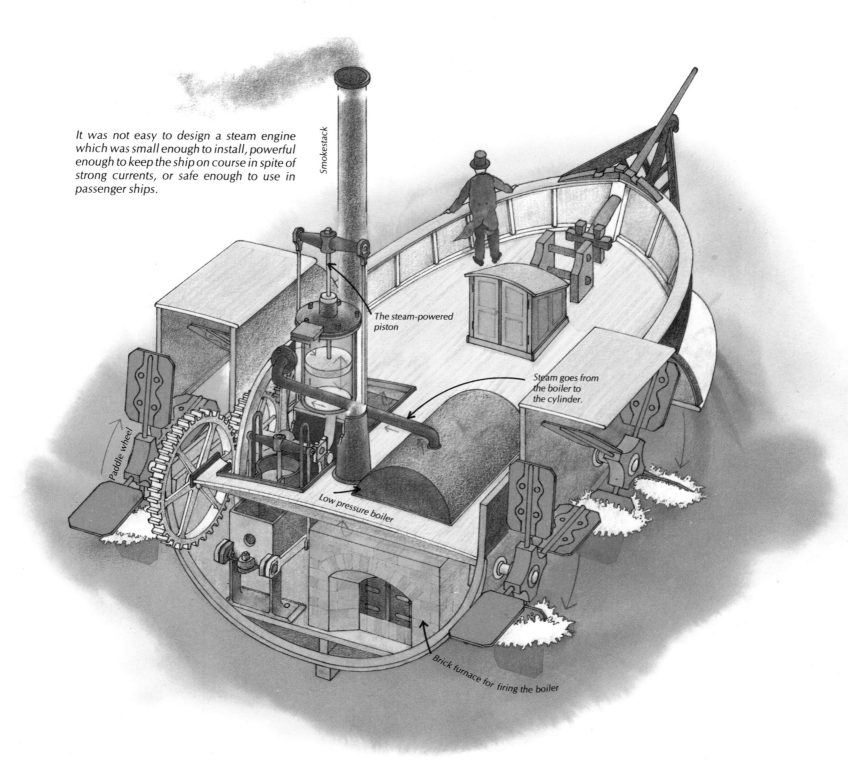

It was not easy to design a steam engine which was small enough to install, powerful enough to keep the ship on course in spite of strong currents, or safe enough to use in passenger ships.

Smokestack

The steam-powered piston

Steam goes from the boiler to the cylinder.

Paddle wheel

Low pressure boiler

Brick furnace for firing the boiler

A paddle wheel works most efficiently when its paddles are pivoted to bite the water.

The pivoted paddles generate the maximum force as the paddle wheel turns.

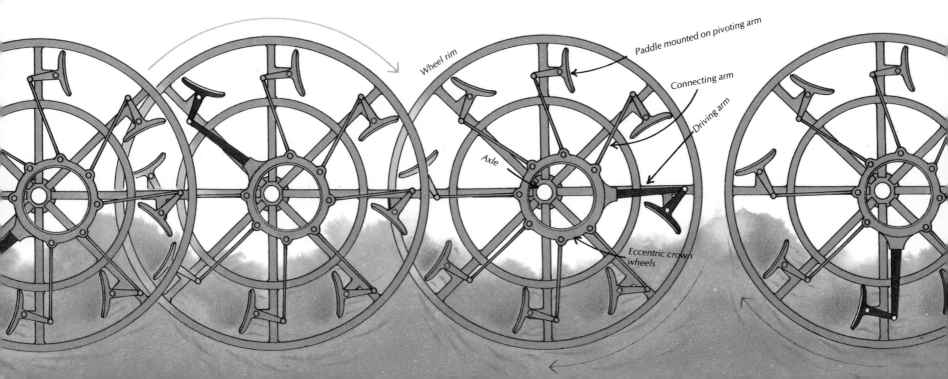

Wheel rim

Paddle mounted on pivoting arm

Connecting arm

Driving arm

Axle

Eccentric crown wheels

Propellers

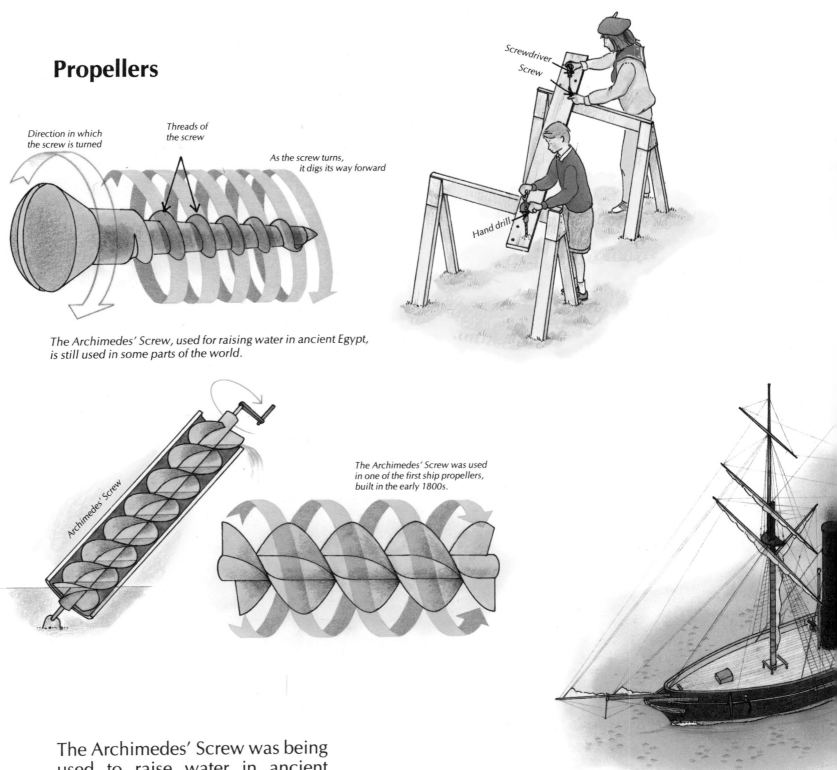

Direction in which the screw is turned

Threads of the screw

As the screw turns, it digs its way forward

The Archimedes' Screw, used for raising water in ancient Egypt, is still used in some parts of the world.

Screwdriver

Screw

Hand drill

Archimedes' Screw

The Archimedes' Screw was used in one of the first ship propellers, built in the early 1800s.

The Archimedes' Screw was being used to raise water in ancient Egypt, four thousand years ago. It was enclosed in a close fitting, watertight cylinder. The machine was turned by hand, and as the screw rotated, water was wound up it and spilled out at the top.

A propeller works like a screw, or like the bit of a drill, digging its way forwards as it spins. Today almost all ships are driven by propellers.

Which was better, a paddle or a propeller? The argument started in 1816, when the first propeller-driven ship was built, and went on until 1845, when the Admiralty held a contest between HMS *Rattler*, which was propeller-driven, and HMS *Alecto*, a paddle-sloop. The ships were tied together, stern to stern, and then the signal to start was given. *Rattler* towed *Alecto* astern, winning the tug of war every time.

The Admiralty meant to be fair. They chose two ships of about the same size, and staged the race in calm water. But it is right to add that the moment of starting is always the moment of least efficiency where paddle wheels are concerned.

HMS Alecto

HMS Rattler

Modern propellers may have two, three, four, five or more blades. They are designed for maximum efficiency. The shape of the blades is designed to suit the work they have to do.

The number and the shape of the blades in a marine propeller depend on the speed and purpose for which the ship is designed.

A propeller for a merchant or passenger ship, which is not likely to achieve very high speeds, has fewer and broader blades.

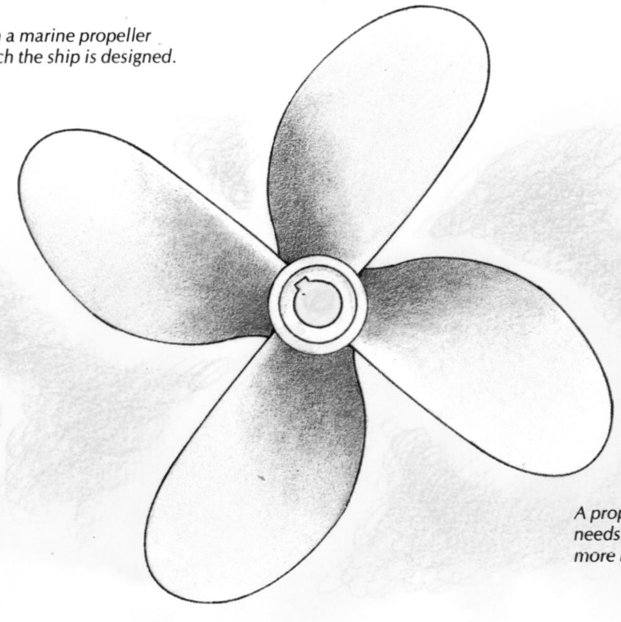

A propeller for a warship, which needs to reach high speeds, has more blades, and they are slimmer.

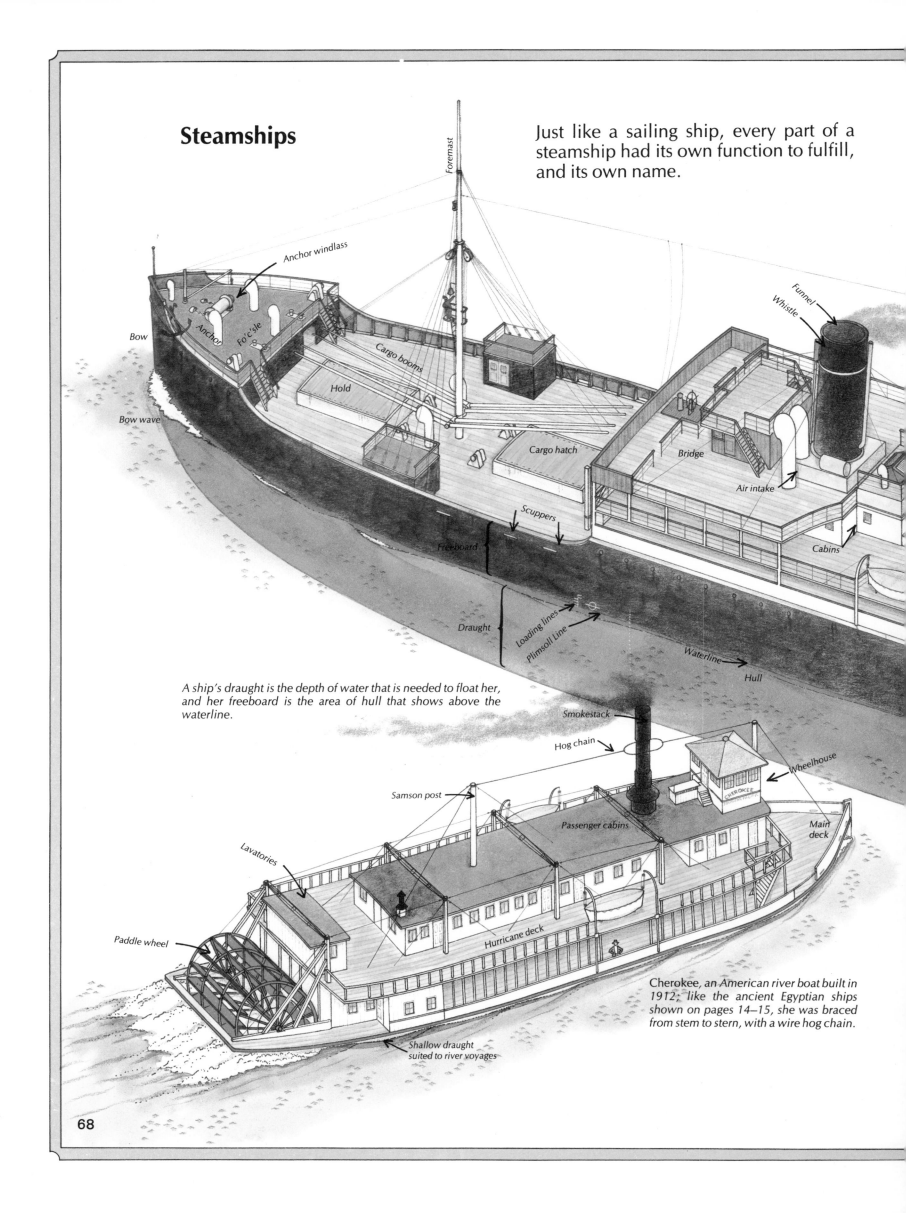

Steamships

Just like a sailing ship, every part of a steamship had its own function to fulfill, and its own name.

Foremast

Anchor windlass

Bow

Anchor

Fo'c'sle

Cargo booms

Bow wave

Hold

Funnel

Whistle

Cargo hatch

Bridge

Air intake

Cabins

Scuppers

Freeboard

Draught

Loading lines

Plimsoll Line

Waterline

Hull

A ship's draught is the depth of water that is needed to float her, and her freeboard is the area of hull that shows above the waterline.

Smokestack

Hog chain

Wheelhouse

Samson post

Passenger cabins

Main deck

Lavatories

Paddle wheel

Hurricane deck

Cherokee, an American river boat built in 1912; like the ancient Egyptian ships shown on pages 14–15, she was braced from stem to stern, with a wire hog chain.

Shallow draught suited to river voyages

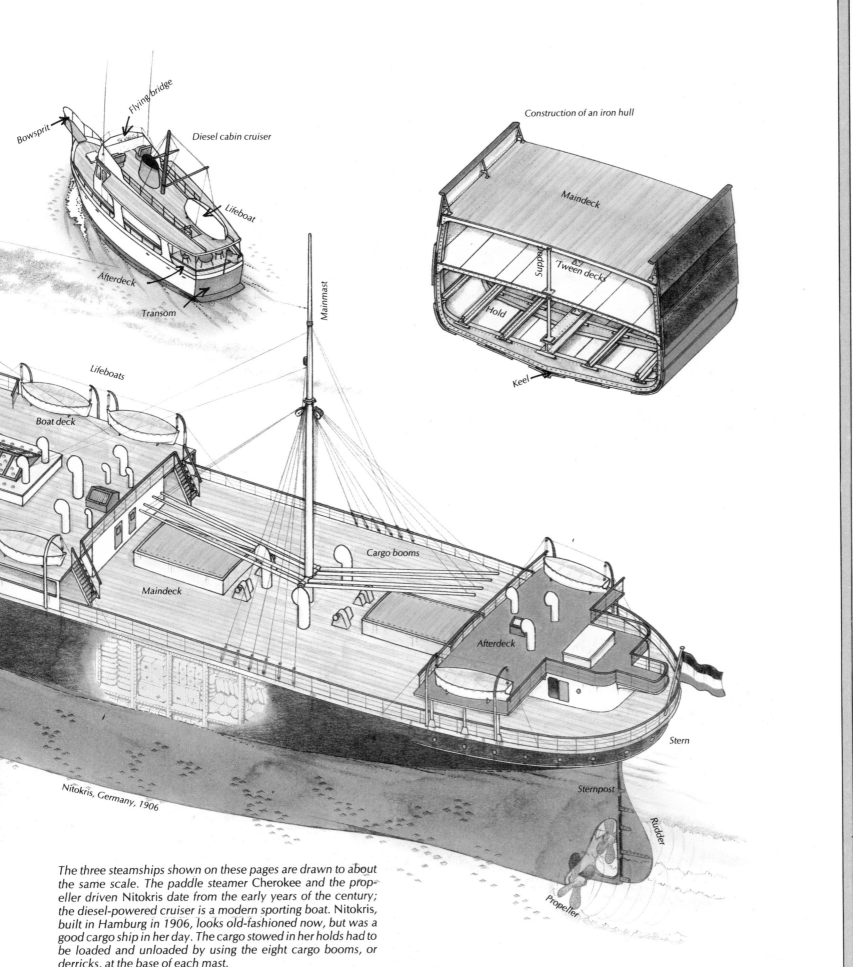

Bowsprit

Flying bridge

Diesel cabin cruiser

Lifeboat

Afterdeck

Transom

Construction of an iron hull

Maindeck

Support

'Tween decks

Hold

Keel

Lifeboats

Boat deck

Mainmast

Cargo booms

Maindeck

Afterdeck

Stern

Sternpost

Rudder

Nitokris, Germany, 1906

Propeller

The three steamships shown on these pages are drawn to about the same scale. The paddle steamer Cherokee and the propeller driven Nitokris date from the early years of the century; the diesel-powered cruiser is a modern sporting boat. Nitokris, built in Hamburg in 1906, looks old-fashioned now, but was a good cargo ship in her day. The cargo stowed in her holds had to be loaded and unloaded by using the eight cargo booms, or derricks, at the base of each mast.

69

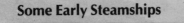

The Pyroscaphe was built in France in 1783, with a steam engine designed by James Watt. Her owner, the Marquis Claude Jouffroy d'Abbans, sailed her up the River Saone, against the current, for a quarter of an hour, but could still not find any backers.

Pyroscaphe, France, 1783

The Comet, built in Glasgow in 1812, was the first European paddle steamer to carry passengers. Her smokestack doubled as a mast, so that she could hoist a sail when the wind was favorable.

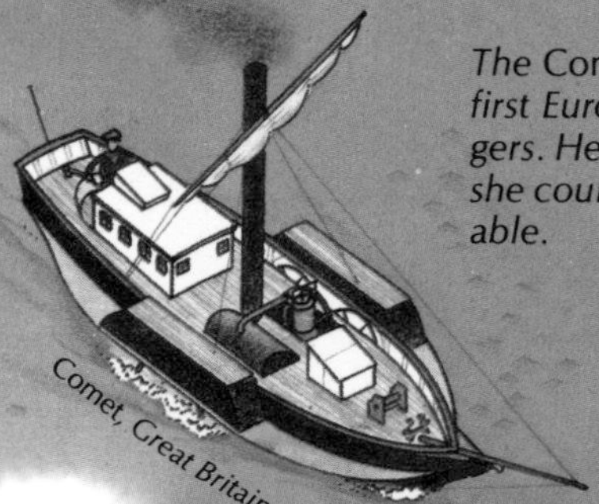

Comet, Great Britain, 1812

Robert Fulton designed and built North River of Clermont, and in 1807 sailed her up the Hudson River from New York to Albany (150 miles, or 240 km), in 32 hours. He set up the world's first successful passenger steamboat service.

North River of Clermont, USA, 1807

Sirius was the first ship to cross the Atlantic by steam power alone—but only just! In the spring of 1837 she sailed from Ireland to New York in 18½ days, but finished the voyage so short of fuel that the crew had to chop and burn the spars.

Sirius, Great Britain, 1837

Miller & Symington's
first steamboat, 1788

The Savannah, built in 1818, was the first ship to make use of steam power on a trans-atlantic crossing. It took her four weeks to sail from Savannah, in the American South, to Liverpool, England, using steam powered paddle wheels to supplement her sails when necessary.

Patrick Miller and William Symington built their first small steamboat in Scotland in 1788. Like many modern yachts, she was a catamaran, with twin hulls. She had two paddle wheels, sandwiched between the hulls, one in front of the other. Fourteen years later they built the Charlotte Dundas for Lord Dundas of Kerse, to tow barges on the Forth & Clyde Canal. She too, was twin-hulled, with the boiler in one hull, the engine in the other, and a single paddle wheel in between.

Charlotte Dundas,
Great Britain, 1802

Savannah, USA, 1818

The Far West is typical of the elegant, flat-bottomed paddle steamers that sailed the Mississippi River at the start of this century. They were nicknamed the river queens. Like many of her sister ships, Far West was eventually destroyed by fire.

FAR WEST

Far West, USA, early 1900s

Cunard's transatlantic ocean liner Mauretania was nicknamed "the Grand Old Lady of the Atlantic." Between 1907 and 1934, she made over 260 double crossings of the Atlantic, and was the fastest liner of her day.

Mauretania, Great Britain, 1907

Uri, Switzerland, 1901

Clemens Sartori, Germany, 1955

Clemens Sartori, a German freighter built in 1955.

Uri, built in 1901, is typical of the passenger paddle steamers used on the Swiss Lakes.

Ferryboats carry passengers, cars and even trains over wide stretches of water. This double-ended paddle wheeler, New York, is typical of many which worked in New York harbor until recently.

New York, USA, 1892

Pusher tugboat

...and barge

BACO-LINER 1

72

The freighter Iberia was typical of many built at the end of the 19th century. She had two masts, so that she could use sail power to supplement her engines.

Iberia, Spain, 1881

Container ships like this one carry different cargoes in separate, sealed containers, which are much easier to load and unload. This ship can carry over 500 containers, as well as 12 barges.

Baco-Liner 1, Germany

BACO-LINER

Dredgers scoop up mud and silt, to keep navigable channels clear. This is an old bucket dredger.

Dredger,   Germany, 1904

Lightships mark dangerous shoals and reefs, and act as weather stations.

BLUNTS

Blunt's Reef, lightship, moored off Cape Mendocino, California

Warships, 1765 to 1969

The USS Constitution, launched in Boston in 1797, proved to be such a fine fighting ship that she was nicknamed "Old Ironsides."

USS Constitution, USA, 1797

HMS Victory, Great Britain, 176

HMS Victory, launched in 1765, was Admiral Nelson's flagship at Trafalgar in 1805, when the British defeated Napoleon's navy; Nelson was wounded during the battle, and died some hours later.

HMS Royal Sovereign, Great Britain, 1892

The seven warships of the Royal Sovereign class, built in the late 19th century, were the first to have steel hulls.

HMS Revenge, Great Britain, 1969

Nuclear submarines, armed with ballistic nuclear missiles, patrol the seas of the world.

The ironclad warships Monitor and Merrimack met in battle on March 9, 1862, during the American Civil War.

USS Monitor, USA (Federal Navy), 1862

CSS Merrimack, renamed Virginia, USA (Confederate Navy), 1862

The German cruiser Nürnberg, built fifty years ago, carried a seaplane which was launched by catapult.

Nurnberg, Germany, 1935

MTB, Germany, 1939–45

Motor torpedo boat from World War II, capable of speeds of 44 mph (72 kmh).

Launched a year after World War II ended, and refitted in 1960, the carrier Eagle was armed with 6 missiles, and carried 30 airplanes and 6 helicopters.

ROS

HMS Eagle, Great Britain, 1946

75

Sailing under Water

Submarines can sail on the surface of the water, but they can also sail beneath it, through the depths of the sea. A submarine has a double hull, with ballast tanks between the inner hull and the outer one. When she is sailing on the surface, her ballast tanks are full of air. If the vent valves are opened, air escapes, and sea water rushes in at the bottom of the tanks. The submarine gets heavier; she displaces more water, and sinks. If the vent valves are closed, and compressed air is blown into the tanks, the sea water is forced out again; the submarine is lighter, and she floats upward. Besides her ballast tanks, she has trim tanks; the amount of water in these is adjusted to keep her balanced.

After hydroplane

Forward hydroplane

1

Air
Ballast tank

Forward hydroplane

Vent valves
Air
Water
Water valves

2

Bottle full of air

Bottle full of water

(1) The submarine floats on the surface of the sea.
(2) The vent valves are opened, and the hydroplanes are tilted to direct the submarine's dive.
(3) The submarine's weight exactly balances the weight of water she displaces; her hydroplanes are horizontal; and she floats in the water.
(4) Compressed air is blown into the tanks; the water is forced out; the hydroplanes are tilted again; and the submarine surfaces.

To test how a submarine works, you need a tank of water and two bottles, each with a cork stopper. A bottle filled with air weighs less than the fluid it displaces, so if you submerge it and then let go, it will rise to the surface again. A bottle filled with water weighs more than the water it displaces, so it sinks.

Periscope
Radio antenna
Conning tower
Bridge
Crew's quarters
Torpedo room
Control deck
Gyroscopic compass
Torpedo tubes

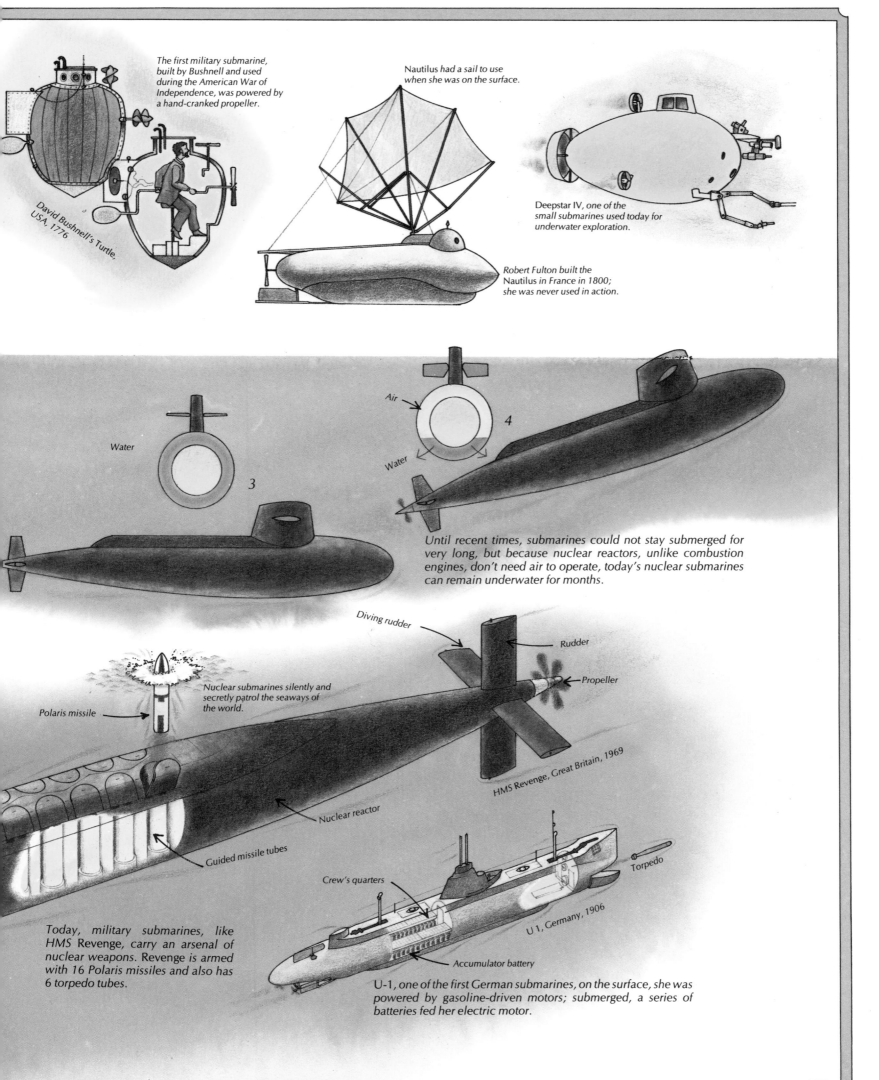

The first military submarine, built by Bushnell and used during the American War of Independence, was powered by a hand-cranked propeller.

David Bushnell's Turtle, USA, 1776

Nautilus had a sail to use when she was on the surface.

Deepstar IV, one of the small submarines used today for underwater exploration.

Robert Fulton built the Nautilus in France in 1800; she was never used in action.

Water

Air

Water

3

4

Until recent times, submarines could not stay submerged for very long, but because nuclear reactors, unlike combustion engines, don't need air to operate, today's nuclear submarines can remain underwater for months.

Diving rudder

Rudder

Propeller

Polaris missile

Nuclear submarines silently and secretly patrol the seaways of the world.

HMS Revenge, Great Britain, 1969

Nuclear reactor

Guided missile tubes

Crew's quarters

Torpedo

U 1, Germany, 1906

Accumulator battery

Today, military submarines, like HMS Revenge, carry an arsenal of nuclear weapons. Revenge is armed with 16 Polaris missiles and also has 6 torpedo tubes.

U-1, one of the first German submarines, on the surface, she was powered by gasoline-driven motors; submerged, a series of batteries fed her electric motor.

77

The upper surface of an airplane's wing is curved so that the air pressure above it is reduced and the greater pressure below lifts it into the air. It is called an airfoil. A hydrofoil works in water in exactly the same way as an airfoil works in air.

Faster air

Slower air

This anti-submarine patrol boat is a hydrofoil craft, whose hydrofoils act like underwater wings. It can travel at 54 knots (60 mph, or 100 kmh).

Torpedo tubes

USS High Point, USA

The hydrofoil wings can be retracted into these housings.

Buffers, to help protect the hydrofoil wings in harbour

Faster water

Forward hydrofoil wing

Slower water

The water flowing faster over the surface of the hydrofoil sucks it upwards.

When the hydrofoil wings are retracted, the propeller can be used to power the boat in the usual way.

Two pairs of propellers are mounted on the rear hydrofoil wings.

Rear hydrofoil wing

Radar

Bridge

Sailing over Water

If a ship is moving slowly through calm water, she slides smoothly along on her hull, and the water offers little resistance; but as the ship begins to pick up speed, the water's resistance increases until it reaches a point at which it is impossible for the ship to go any faster. To overcome the speed limit which is imposed by the water's resistance, modern inventors have designed the hydrofoil. When it is traveling at a slow speed, the hydrofoil floats in the water like any other ship, but as its speed builds up, it is lifted clear of the water by its hydrofoils and skims over the surface.

A hovercraft's fans suck in great quantities of air. Some of the air is used to power the propellers, but the rest of it is blown downward to create a cushion of air between the craft and the water. The hovercraft has a flexible skirt which helps to reduce the loss of air from the cushion, but this still has to be replenished constantly. Hovercraft can also fly across snow and ice, mud and swamp, and fairly level ground; the rougher the surface, the deeper the cushion of air should be.

Forward loading ramp

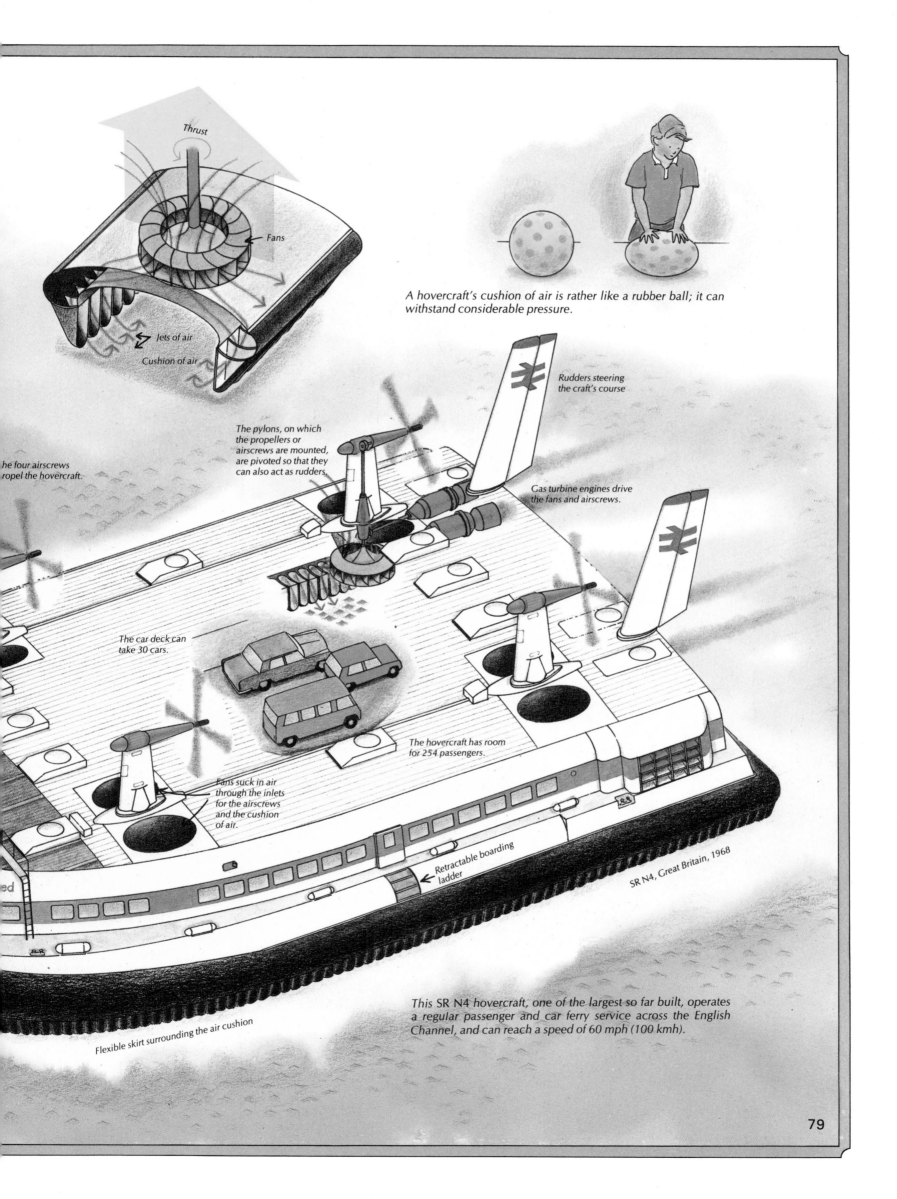

Thrust

Fans

Jets of air

Cushion of air

A hovercraft's cushion of air is rather like a rubber ball; it can withstand considerable pressure.

Rudders steering the craft's course

The pylons, on which the propellers or airscrews are mounted, are pivoted so that they can also act as rudders.

Gas turbine engines drive the fans and airscrews.

he four airscrews ropel the hovercraft.

The car deck can take 30 cars.

The hovercraft has room for 254 passengers.

Fans suck in air through the inlets for the airscrews and the cushion of air.

Retractable boarding ladder

SR N4, Great Britain, 1968

Flexible skirt surrounding the air cushion

This SR N4 hovercraft, one of the largest so far built, operates a regular passenger and car ferry service across the English Channel, and can reach a speed of 60 mph (100 kmh).

Crossing Dry Land

Ships do not only sail the seas. Most of the Earth's continents are drained by great rivers flowing to the sea, and ships can often sail inland, if the river is wide and deep.

As well as the rivers, there are canals which have been dug out and filled with water to make waterways between ports and towns. Ships cannot sail uphill, so wherever rivers or canals cross land that isn't level, systems of locks have been built.

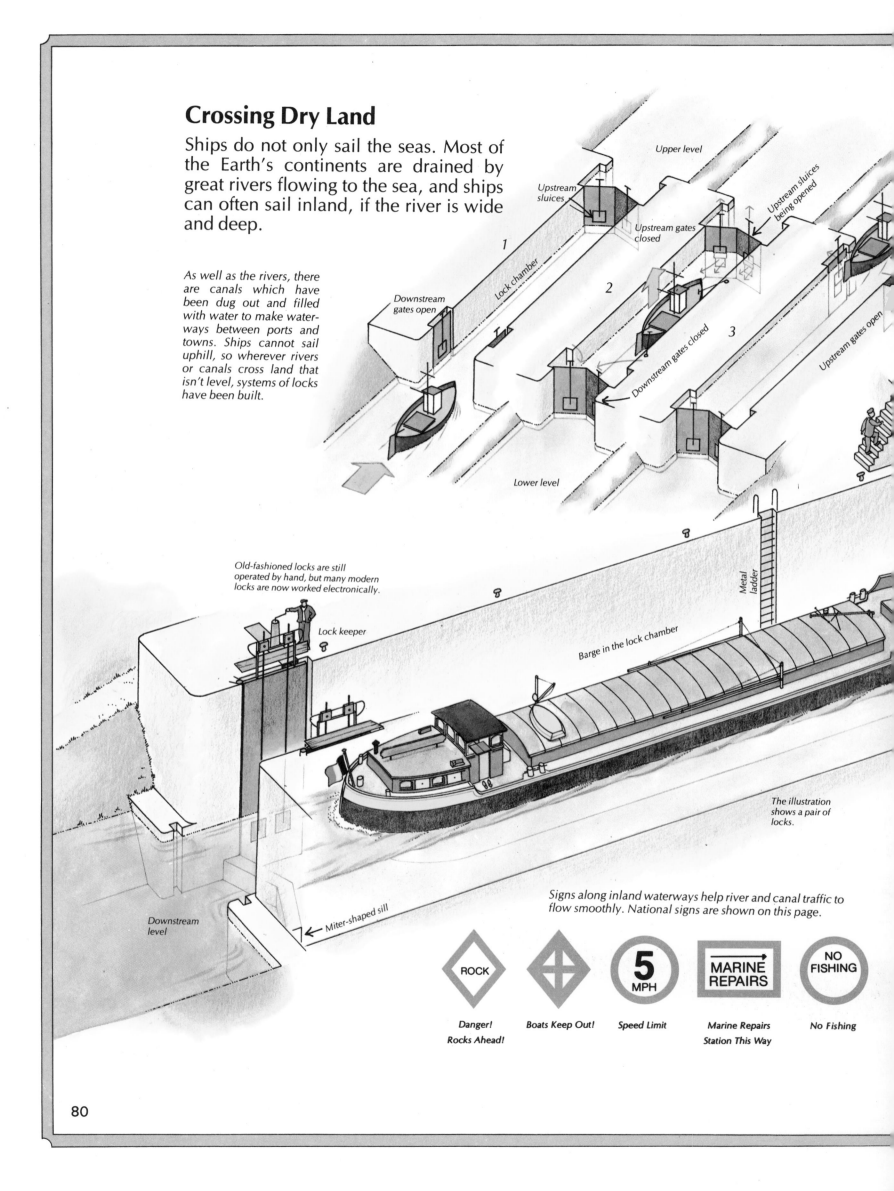

Upper level

Upstream sluices

Upstream gates closed

Upstream sluices being opened

1

Lock chamber

2

Downstream gates open

Downstream gates closed

3

Upstream gates open

Lower level

Old-fashioned locks are still operated by hand, but many modern locks are now worked electronically.

Lock keeper

Metal ladder

Barge in the lock chamber

The illustration shows a pair of locks.

Downstream level

Miter-shaped sill

Signs along inland waterways help river and canal traffic to flow smoothly. National signs are shown on this page.

ROCK

5 MPH

MARINE REPAIRS

NO FISHING

Danger! Rocks Ahead!

Boats Keep Out!

Speed Limit

Marine Repairs Station This Way

No Fishing

The illustration on the left-hand page shows how locks can link waterways at different levels. (1) The boat sails into the lock through the open downstream gates. (2) The gates are closed, and the sluices in the upstream gates are opened so that the lock chamber fills with water and the boat floats upwards. (3) The upstream gates are opened, and the boat sails out on to the upper level.

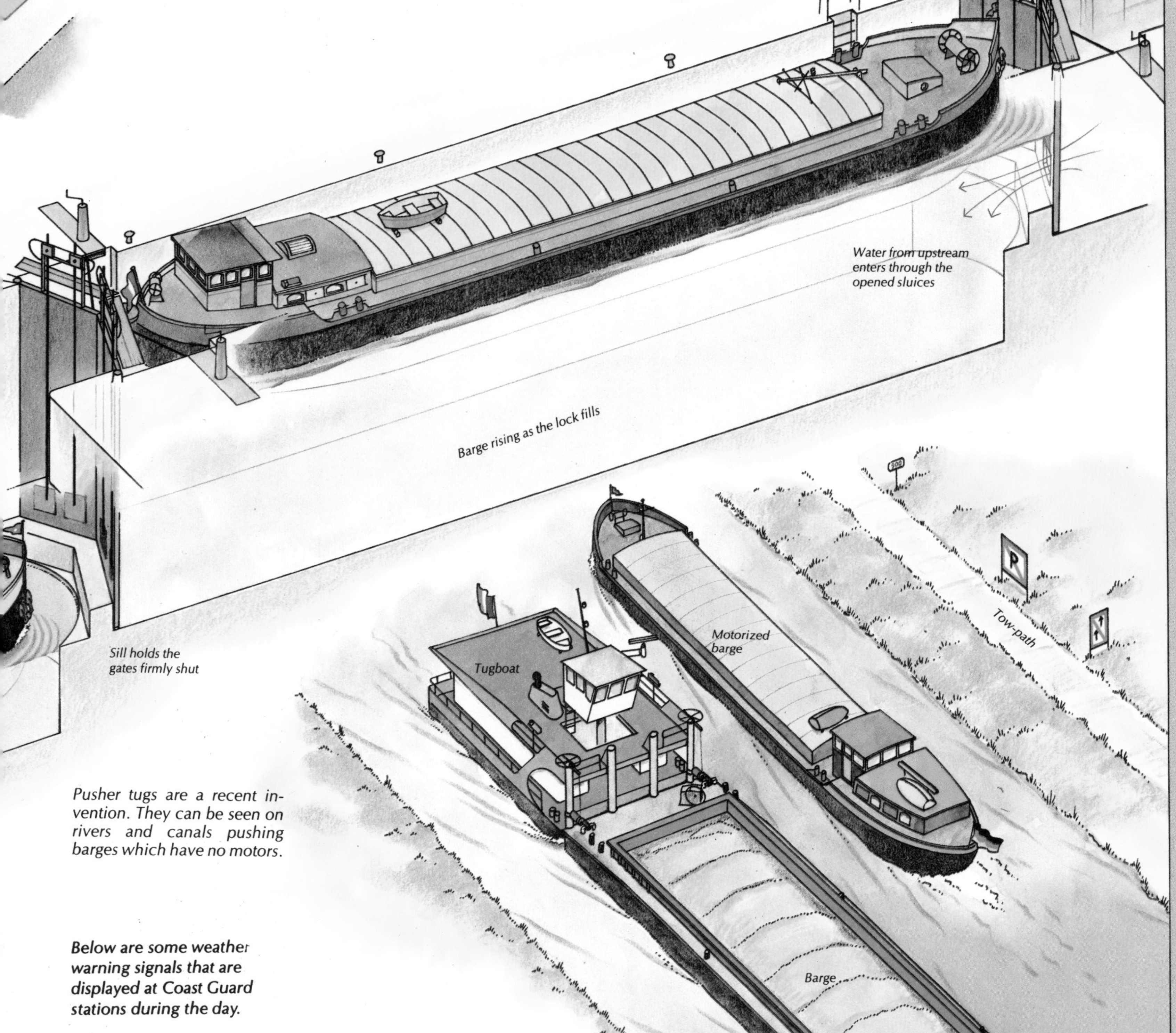

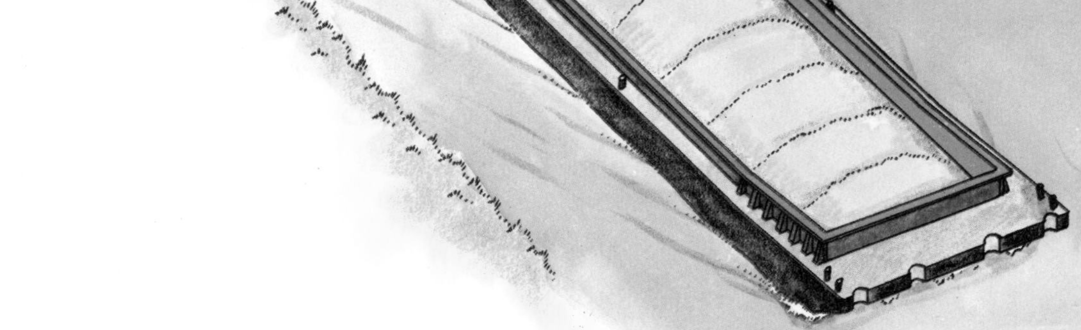

Upstream level

Water from upstream enters through the opened sluices

Barge rising as the lock fills

Sill holds the gates firmly shut

Motorized barge

Tugboat

Tow-path

Pusher tugs are a recent invention. They can be seen on rivers and canals pushing barges which have no motors.

Barge

Below are some weather warning signals that are displayed at Coast Guard stations during the day.

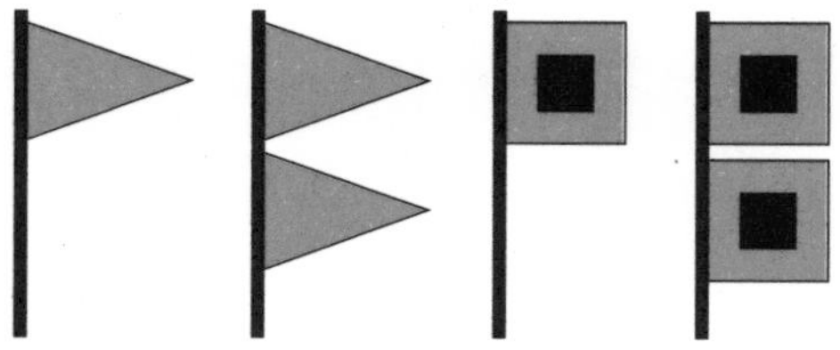

Small Craft Gale Storm Hurricane

Finding the Way

When seamen first ventured into the open sea, out of sight of land, they steered by using the stars. The positions of some stars change hardly at all during the night hours, so if a sailor picked out the Pole Star and kept it at about the same point—say, just to one side of the prow—the ship would sail a straight course all night long. But this didn't work, of course, in bad weather, or by daylight, when men had to rely on the sun as it traveled across the heavens from rising to setting.

At home there are familiar landmarks to help you find your way, street signs you can read, people you can ask. But at sea there are no such aids. Whichever way you look, you can see only sky and water. Sailors find their way by using the science of navigation.

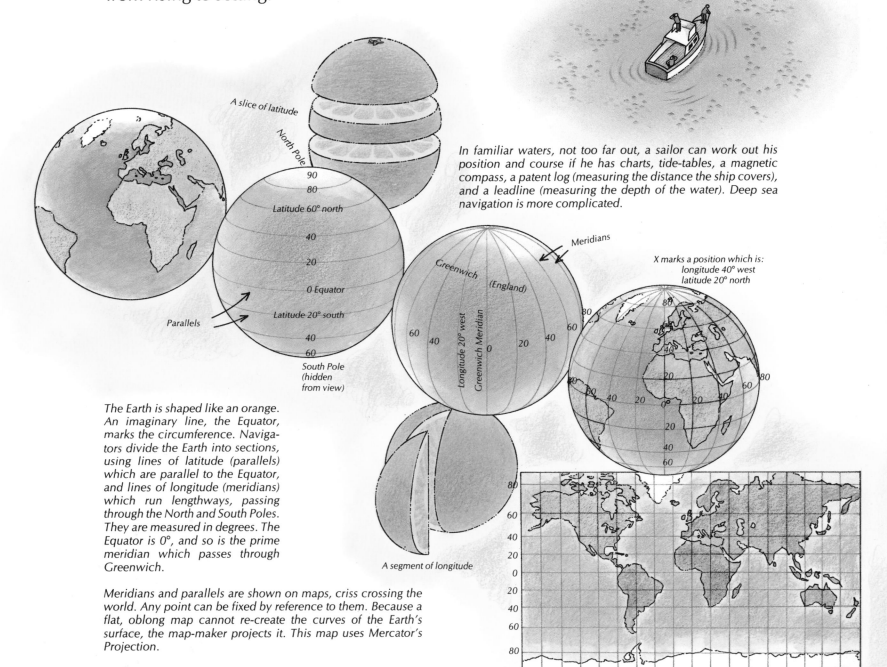

In familiar waters, not too far out, a sailor can work out his position and course if he has charts, tide-tables, a magnetic compass, a patent log (measuring the distance the ship covers), and a leadline (measuring the depth of the water). Deep sea navigation is more complicated.

The Earth is shaped like an orange. An imaginary line, the Equator, marks the circumference. Navigators divide the Earth into sections, using lines of latitude (parallels) which are parallel to the Equator, and lines of longitude (meridians) which run lengthways, passing through the North and South Poles. They are measured in degrees. The Equator is 0°, and so is the prime meridian which passes through Greenwich.

Meridians and parallels are shown on maps, criss crossing the world. Any point can be fixed by reference to them. Because a flat, oblong map cannot re-create the curves of the Earth's surface, the map-maker projects it. This map uses Mercator's Projection.

Because the Earth rotates once in each twenty-four hours, the time of day differs depending on where in the world you are. A navigator needs to know the difference between local time and time at Greenwich. For example, if it is seven o'clock in the morning at Greenwich, and five o'clock in the morning where you are, your longitude is 30° west. The Earth rotates once in twenty-four hours, turning through a complete circle of 360°, so in two hours it will turn 30°.

Clock

The angle of a star above the horizon varies according to the latitude of the observer.

A navigator can fix his latitude by measuring the angle at which a star is above the horizon. This measurement is usually done by using a sextant, which is a very precise instrument. A sextant, charts, mathematical tables, an almanac, a pair of compasses, a pencil and a compass are the tools of the navigator's trade.

Clock

Mirror

Mirror

Telescopic sight

Sextant

120 90 60 30 0

Arc marked in degrees

Movable arm (the alidade)

The Earth itself is a magnet with a magnetic north pole and a magnetic south pole close to (but not at) the North and South Poles. The needle in a magnetic compass is magnetized so that it points towards magnetic north. The navigator using it must allow for the difference between true north and magnetic north. With a modern gyro-compass, this is no longer necessary.

Tables

Compasses

Chart

Pole Star

Great Bear

Magnetic North Pole

North Pole

Magnetic compass

N

W   E

S

Radio transmitter sending out signals which help to fix the ship's position

The lines on a chart show the varying depth of the water close to the coast.

Radar screen

Radar

Modern technology (in particular, electronics) has revolution-ized navigation. Radar, sonar, radio transmitters and satellites orbiting the Earth, have all made navigation faster and more accurate.

Sonar measures the depth of water below the keel.

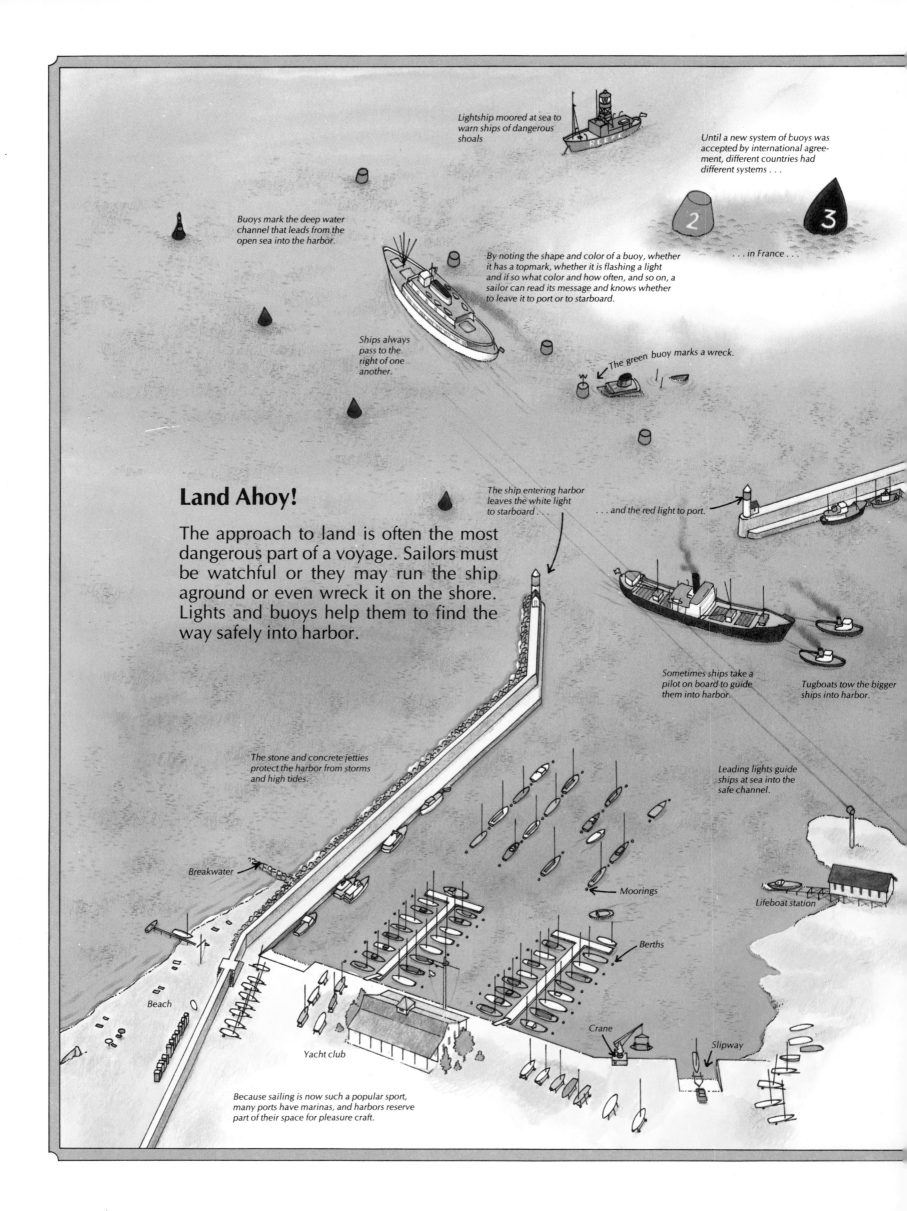

Lightship moored at sea to warn ships of dangerous shoals

Until a new system of buoys was accepted by international agreement, different countries had different systems . . .

Buoys mark the deep water channel that leads from the open sea into the harbor.

By noting the shape and color of a buoy, whether it has a topmark, whether it is flashing a light and if so what color and how often, and so on, a sailor can read its message and knows whether to leave it to port or to starboard.

. . . in France . . .

Ships always pass to the right of one another.

The green buoy marks a wreck.

Land Ahoy!

The ship entering harbor leaves the white light to starboard . . .

. . . and the red light to port.

The approach to land is often the most dangerous part of a voyage. Sailors must be watchful or they may run the ship aground or even wreck it on the shore. Lights and buoys help them to find the way safely into harbor.

Sometimes ships take a pilot on board to guide them into harbor.

Tugboats tow the bigger ships into harbor.

The stone and concrete jetties protect the harbor from storms and high tides.

Leading lights guide ships at sea into the safe channel.

Breakwater

Moorings

Lifeboat station

Berths

Beach

Crane

Slipway

Yacht club

Because sailing is now such a popular sport, many ports have marinas, and harbors reserve part of their space for pleasure craft.

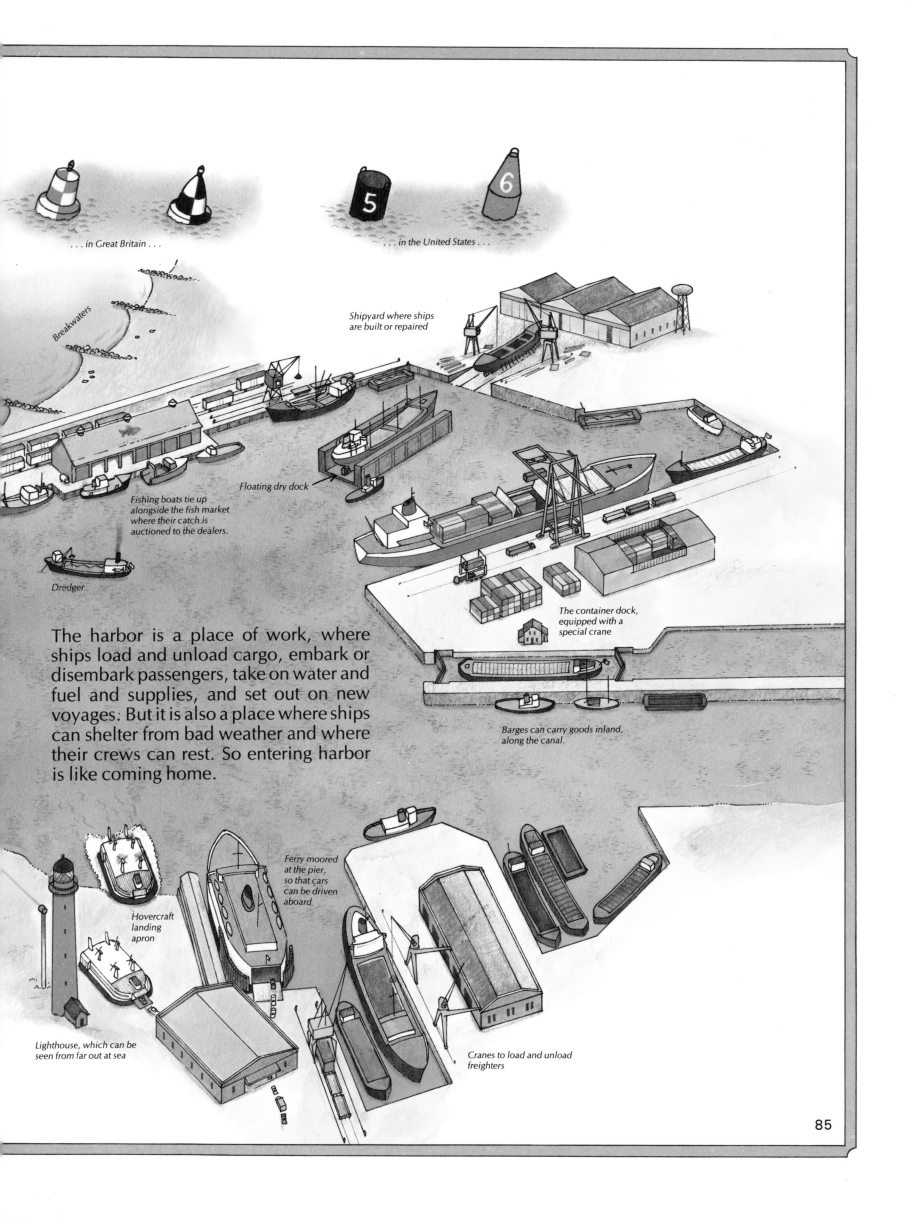

. . . in Great Britain . . .

. . . in the United States . . .

Breakwaters

Shipyard where ships
are built or repaired

Fishing boats tie up
alongside the fish market
where their catch is
auctioned to the dealers.

Floating dry dock

Dredger

The harbor is a place of work, where
ships load and unload cargo, embark or
disembark passengers, take on water and
fuel and supplies, and set out on new
voyages. But it is also a place where ships
can shelter from bad weather and where
their crews can rest. So entering harbor
is like coming home.

The container dock,
equipped with a
special crane

Barges can carry goods inland,
along the canal.

Ferry moored
at the pier,
so that cars
can be driven
aboard

Hovercraft
landing
apron

Lighthouse, which can be
seen from far out at sea

Cranes to load and unload
freighters

Things that
Fly

The Ocean of Air

Air is all around us. Whichever way we turn, and reaching high above our heads, there is air. The entire Earth is surrounded by a sphere of air, called the atmosphere, so vast and deep that it is sometimes nicknamed the Ocean of Air.

Mount Everest
the highest point on Earth
29,028 ft (8,848 m)

Mont Blanc
the highest point in the Alps
15,771 ft (4,807 m)

Eiffel Tower, Paris
1,050 ft (320 m)

Modern jet airliners cruise
at altitudes in the region
of 20,000–40,000 ft (6,000–12,000 m)

9,000 m
8,000 m
7,000 m
6,000 m
5,000 m
4,000 m
3,000 m
2,000 m
1,000 meters
Sea level

In 1963 the American experimental rocket aircraft X-15 reached over 350,650 ft (107,000 m), well into space!

The stratosphere lies above the troposphere. Modern jet aircraft fly in this less dense layer of the atmosphere.

The U-2 spy plane could fly at about 65,500 ft (20,000 m).

In 1935 the American balloon Explorer II, piloted by Captain Anderson and Captain Stevens, rose to over 72,000 ft (22,000 m).

Professor Piccard was the first man to reach the stratosphere. In 1932 his balloon, the FNRS, rose to over 52,500 ft (16,000 m).

^ Stratosphere
Troposphere ∨

Concorde can cruise at altitudes of up to over 62,000 ft (19,000 m).

22,000 m
21,000 m
20,000 m
19,000 m
18,000 m
17,000 m
16,000 m
15,000 m
14,000 m
13,000 m
12,000 m
11,000 m
10,000 m
9,000 m
8,000 m
7,000 m
6,000 m
5,000 m
4,000 m
3,000 m

5,000 m
6,000 m
7,000 m
8,000 m
9,000 m
10,000 m
11,000 m
12,000 m

Like the oceans on Earth, the Ocean of Air gets denser the deeper you go. We live at the bottom of the atmosphere, in its densest layer, called the troposphere. It is in the troposphere that weather occurs. We walk at the bottom of the Ocean of Air, like the crabs that crawl on the sea bed. Birds, balloons and airplanes fly through the air with the same ease as fish swim in the sea. How do they fly? It is, above all, thanks to the Ocean of Air itself that flight through it is possible.

Lighter Than Air

Have you ever watched smoke rise from a fire? It seems to be lighter than air as it rises into the sky. Heat has an interesting effect on air. It excites it, making the particles move about furiously. Because each particle then needs more space to move in, the effect is to expand the air.

As there are fewer particles in hot air than cold air, hot air really does become lighter than cold. Smoke and ashes do indeed ride a hot wind skyward through a sea of cooler, heavier air.

Slow particles

Cold air

Fast particles

Hot air

Two hundred years ago, two brothers living in France, Joseph Michel and Jacques Etienne Montgolfier, were puzzled by smoke's ability to rise. They wondered if it would be possible to use rising smoke to lift something. They held a light, silken bag over a fire and watched it fill with smoke. After a while, it billowed, and tugged . . . lifting like magic into the air!

Encouraged by the success of their first experiments at home, the Montgolfier brothers made a big, spherical bag with sections of paper and cloth held together by buttons. They sent this balloon aloft in their home town of Annonay on June 5, 1783. The magical sight of the balloon defying gravity not only amazed the witnesses but also excited the curiosity of the whole world. It marked the beginning of the history of flight.

Balloons filled with hydrogen or helium gas (both are lighter than air) rise through the atmosphere as easily as bubbles through water.

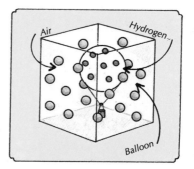

At a fair you can sometimes buy toy balloons. They are not filled with hot air but with a gas (usually helium) whose particles weigh less than those of the air. The balloons will escape from you quickly if you don't hold the string tightly.

Hot Air or Gas

The Montgolfiers' experiments with hot air two hundred years ago, led to the invention of balloons that could carry men. Within a few months of the Annonay flight, two different types of balloon, one filled with hot air, the other with hydrogen (a gas recently discovered by the English scientist Henry Cavendish), had appeared in the sky above Paris.

When news of the Montgolfiers' experiments reached the King of France, Louis XVI, he immediately asked them to send off a balloon from his palace at Versailles.

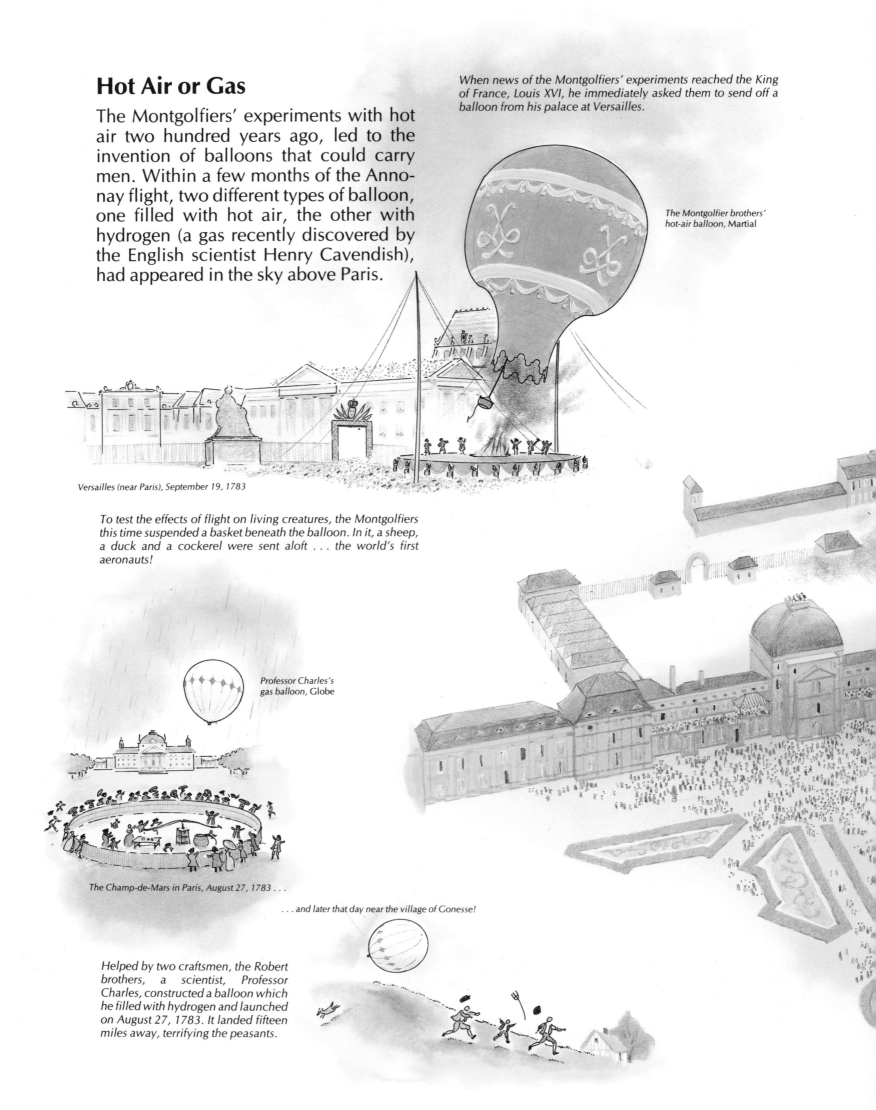

The Montgolfier brothers' hot-air balloon, Martial

Versailles (near Paris), September 19, 1783

To test the effects of flight on living creatures, the Montgolfiers this time suspended a basket beneath the balloon. In it, a sheep, a duck and a cockerel were sent aloft . . . the world's first aeronauts!

Professor Charles's gas balloon, Globe

The Champ-de-Mars in Paris, August 27, 1783 . . .

. . . and later that day near the village of Gonesse!

Helped by two craftsmen, the Robert brothers, a scientist, Professor Charles, constructed a balloon which he filled with hydrogen and launched on August 27, 1783. It landed fifteen miles away, terrifying the peasants.

Flight over Paris in the Montgolfière balloon, November 21, 1783

Two months after the animal aeronauts had been brought down safely, two brave men, François Pilâtre de Rozier and the Marquis d'Arlandes, made a daring flight over the rooftops of Paris in the biggest balloon the Montgolfiers had yet built. Ten days later, Jacques Charles and Noël Robert ascended in a gas-filled balloon from the Tuileries gardens in Paris before an enormous crowd.

Pilâtre de Rozier and d'Arlandes had to stoke the fire burning at the mouth of the balloon.

Flight from the Tuileries gardens in the Charlière balloon, December 1, 1783

The hydrogen balloon carried Jacques Charles and Noël Robert twenty-seven miles from the French capital. The gas-filled Charlière was much easier to fly, and stayed aloft longer, than the hot-air Montgolfière.

Ballooning

A balloon is at the mercy of the winds and the weather, and piloting it skillfully is largely a matter of balancing the craft against air currents and weather conditions. Because hydrogen gas has a greater lifting power than the same volume of hot air, the envelope of a hot-air balloon (red and yellow stripes in the illustrations) must be much bigger than that of a gas-filled balloon (pink and white stripes).

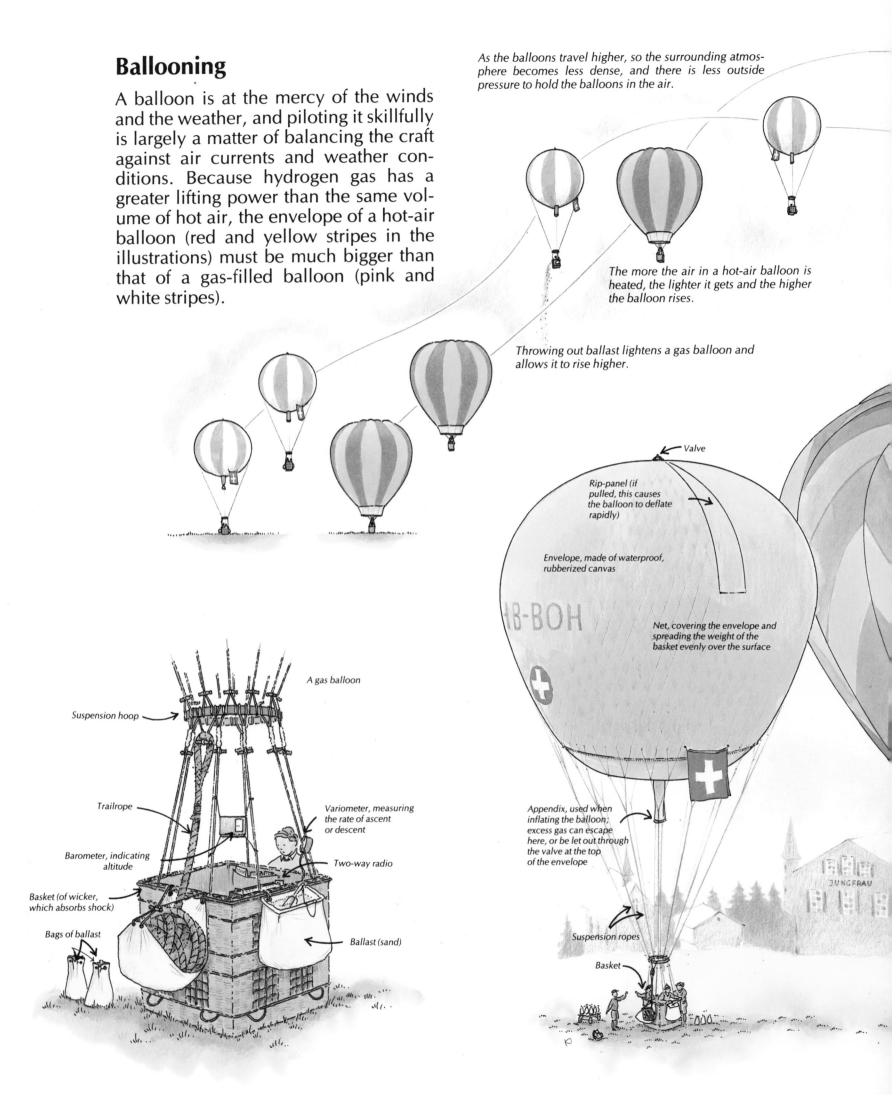

As the balloons travel higher, so the surrounding atmosphere becomes less dense, and there is less outside pressure to hold the balloons in the air.

The more the air in a hot-air balloon is heated, the lighter it gets and the higher the balloon rises.

Throwing out ballast lightens a gas balloon and allows it to rise higher.

A gas balloon

Suspension hoop

Trailrope

Variometer, measuring the rate of ascent or descent

Barometer, indicating altitude

Two-way radio

Basket (of wicker, which absorbs shock)

Bags of ballast

Ballast (sand)

Valve

Rip-panel (if pulled, this causes the balloon to deflate rapidly)

Envelope, made of waterproof, rubberized canvas

HB-BOH

Net, covering the envelope and spreading the weight of the basket evenly over the surface

Appendix, used when inflating the balloon; excess gas can escape here, or be let out through the valve at the top of the envelope

Suspension ropes

Basket

JUNGFRAU

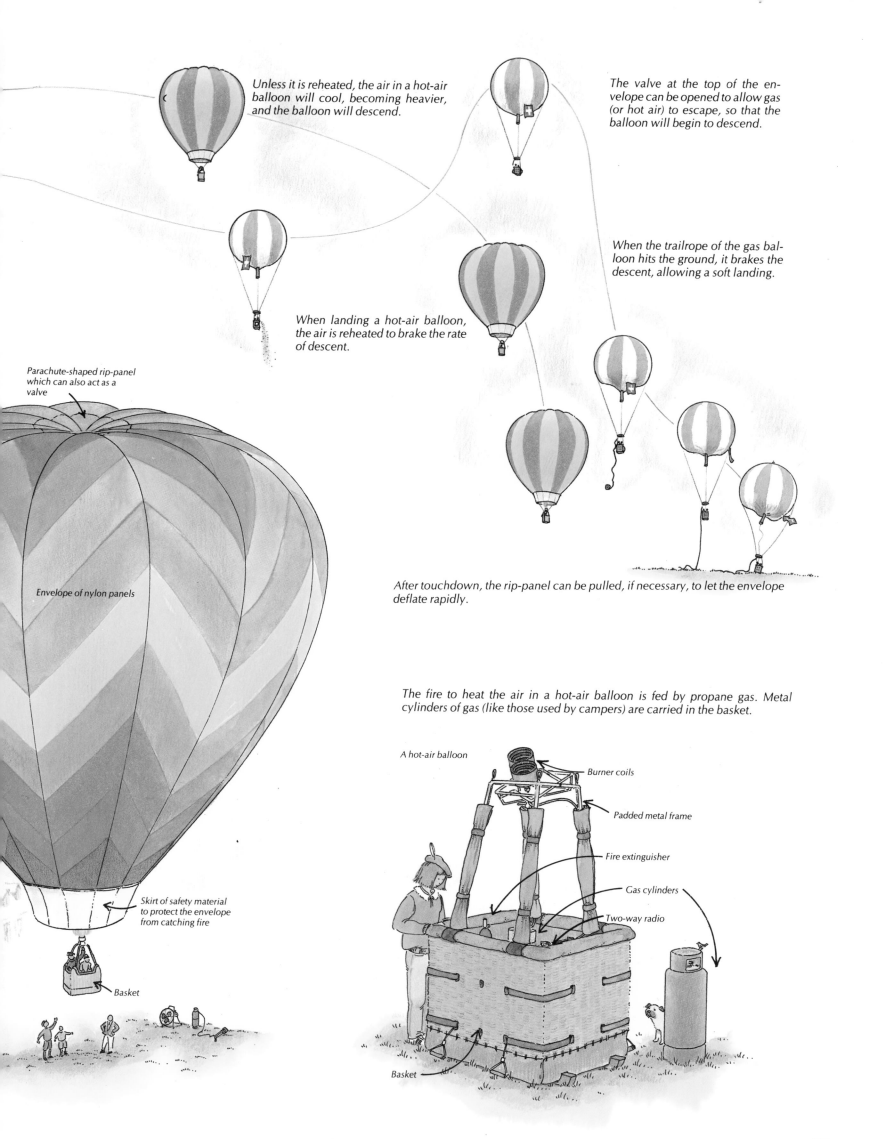

Unless it is reheated, the air in a hot-air balloon will cool, becoming heavier, and the balloon will descend.

The valve at the top of the envelope can be opened to allow gas (or hot air) to escape, so that the balloon will begin to descend.

When the trailrope of the gas balloon hits the ground, it brakes the descent, allowing a soft landing.

When landing a hot-air balloon, the air is reheated to brake the rate of descent.

Parachute-shaped rip-panel which can also act as a valve

Envelope of nylon panels

After touchdown, the rip-panel can be pulled, if necessary, to let the envelope deflate rapidly.

The fire to heat the air in a hot-air balloon is fed by propane gas. Metal cylinders of gas (like those used by campers) are carried in the basket.

A hot-air balloon

Burner coils

Padded metal frame

Fire extinguisher

Gas cylinders

Two-way radio

Skirt of safety material to protect the envelope from catching fire

Basket

Basket

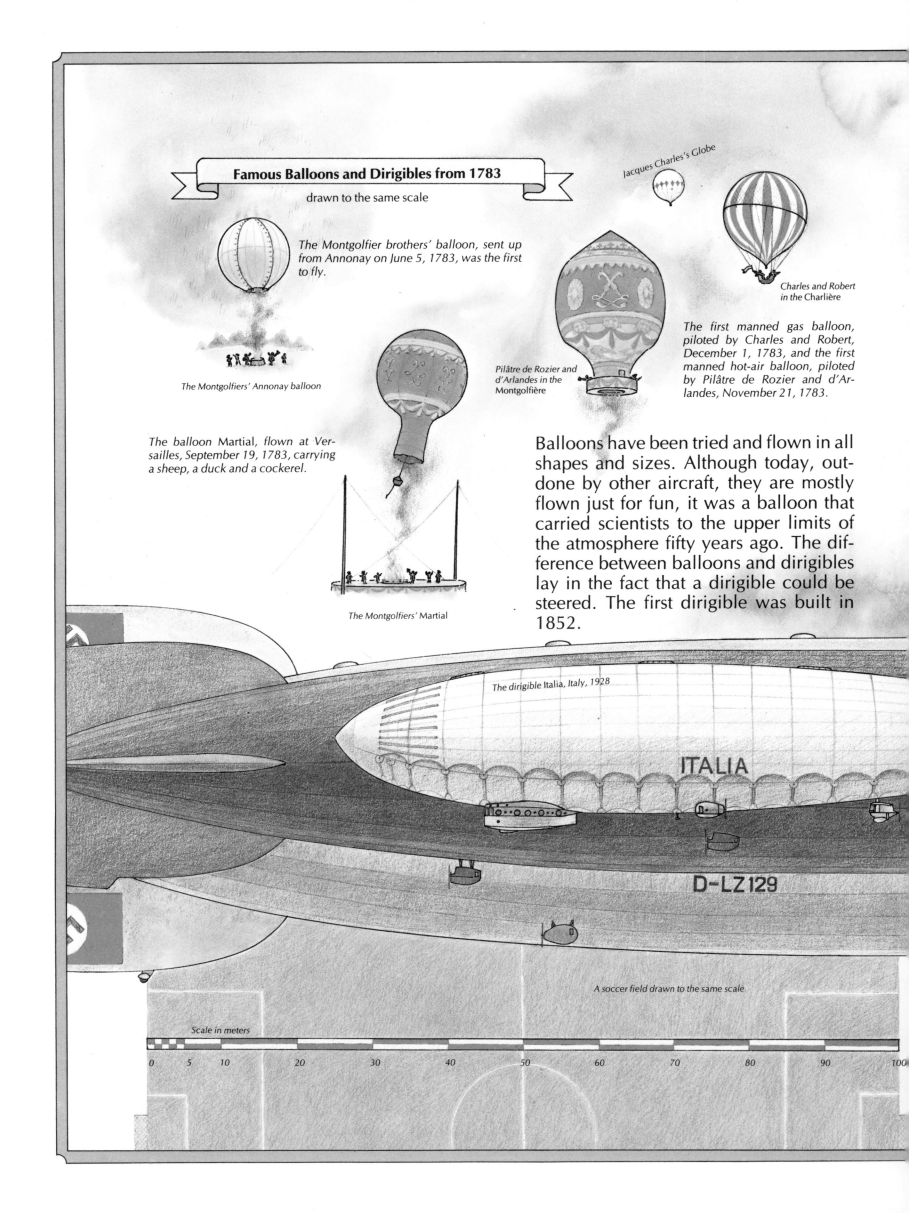

Famous Balloons and Dirigibles from 1783

drawn to the same scale

Jacques Charles's Globe

The Montgolfier brothers' balloon, sent up from Annonay on June 5, 1783, was the first to fly.

The Montgolfiers' Annonay balloon

Charles and Robert in the Charlière

Pilâtre de Rozier and d'Arlandes in the Montgolfière

The first manned gas balloon, piloted by Charles and Robert, December 1, 1783, and the first manned hot-air balloon, piloted by Pilâtre de Rozier and d'Arlandes, November 21, 1783.

The balloon Martial, *flown at Versailles, September 19, 1783, carrying a sheep, a duck and a cockerel.*

The Montgolfiers' Martial

Balloons have been tried and flown in all shapes and sizes. Although today, outdone by other aircraft, they are mostly flown just for fun, it was a balloon that carried scientists to the upper limits of the atmosphere fifty years ago. The difference between balloons and dirigibles lay in the fact that a dirigible could be steered. The first dirigible was built in 1852.

The dirigible Italia, Italy, 1928

ITALIA

D-LZ 129

A soccer field drawn to the same scale

Scale in meters

0   5   10   20   30   40   50   60   70   80   90   100

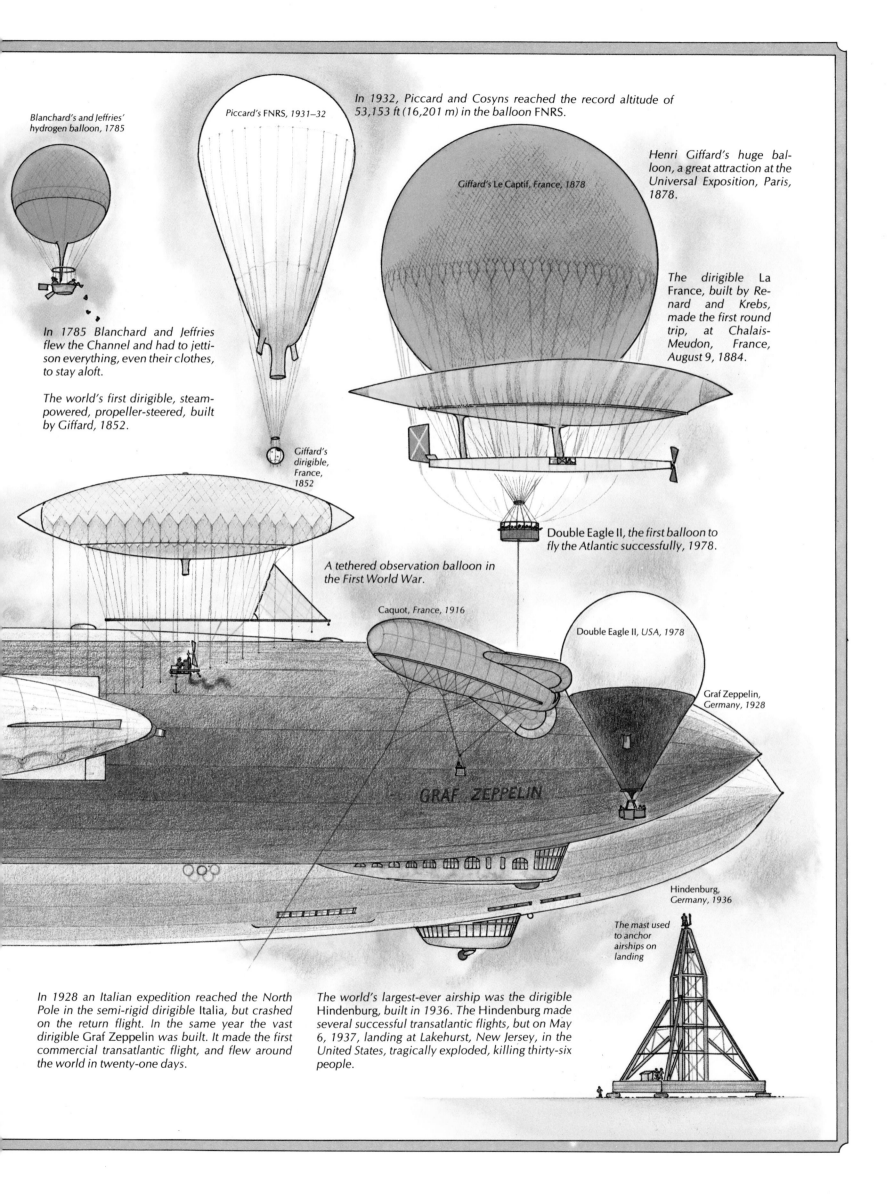

Blanchard's and Jeffries' hydrogen balloon, 1785

Piccard's FNRS, 1931–32

In 1932, Piccard and Cosyns reached the record altitude of 53,153 ft (16,201 m) in the balloon FNRS.

Giffard's Le Captif, France, 1878

Henri Giffard's huge balloon, a great attraction at the Universal Exposition, Paris, 1878.

In 1785 Blanchard and Jeffries flew the Channel and had to jettison everything, even their clothes, to stay aloft.

The world's first dirigible, steam-powered, propeller-steered, built by Giffard, 1852.

Giffard's dirigible, France, 1852

The dirigible La France, built by Renard and Krebs, made the first round trip, at Chalais-Meudon, France, August 9, 1884.

A tethered observation balloon in the First World War.

Double Eagle II, the first balloon to fly the Atlantic successfully, 1978.

Caquot, France, 1916

Double Eagle II, USA, 1978

Graf Zeppelin, Germany, 1928

GRAF ZEPPELIN

Hindenburg, Germany, 1936

The mast used to anchor airships on landing

In 1928 an Italian expedition reached the North Pole in the semi-rigid dirigible Italia, but crashed on the return flight. In the same year the vast dirigible Graf Zeppelin was built. It made the first commercial transatlantic flight, and flew around the world in twenty-one days.

The world's largest-ever airship was the dirigible Hindenburg, built in 1936. The Hindenburg made several successful transatlantic flights, but on May 6, 1937, landing at Lakehurst, New Jersey, in the United States, tragically exploded, killing thirty-six people.

Heavier Than Air

Unlike balloons, which are lighter than air, most things that fly are heavier than air. How do they do it? While apples plummet with a thud, autumn leaves slide gently to the ground. They are thin and flat, and ride on the back of the air particles beneath them. Leaves, kites and parachutes, all fly in this way.

Drawing by Leonardo da Vinci, 1514

Although the Italian artist Leonardo da Vinci drew designs for a parachute nearly five hundred years ago, the first man to put the idea into practice was André Jacques Garnerin.

Garnerin attached his parachute to the basket of a balloon, and on October 22, 1797, at a height of 1,000 meters above Paris, cut the suspension ropes and used the parachute to make a safe landing.

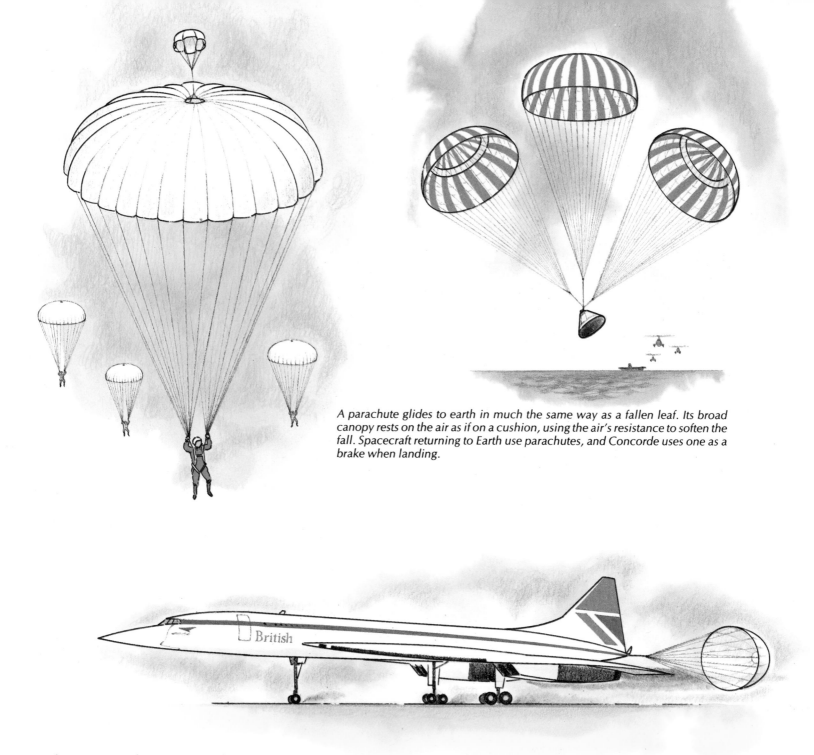

A parachute glides to earth in much the same way as a fallen leaf. Its broad canopy rests on the air as if on a cushion, using the air's resistance to soften the fall. Spacecraft returning to Earth use parachutes, and Concorde uses one as a brake when landing.

The atmosphere is made up of myriads of particles, which resist anything passing through the air. You can feel this resistance when you ride a bicycle, for instance. Given the right shape, an object can glide through the air, catching the air particles beneath it and sliding over them.

Drop a flat sheet of paper, and it will glide down through the air. Crumple it so that it cannot catch the air particles beneath it, and it falls straight to the ground. Toss a crumpled sheet of paper into the air, and it arches to the earth. Fold it properly, and it glides like a bird!

Birds

To glide earthward through the air is one thing. To propel yourself masterfully through it is quite another! Birds are nature's ultimate flying-machines. A good many insects are also able to fly. Of course, it is the bird's wings that enable it to fly. But wings alone are not enough.

Every part of a bird is adapted to flying. Its wings are aerodynamically shaped. Pushing against the air's resistance with a powerful downstroke of the wing moves the bird forwards. As it lifts its wings again, the outer feathers separate so that there is minimum resistance during the upstroke. At full upstroke they fold into a broad, smooth sweep of wing, ready for another powerful thrust downward. Different types of wing suit different styles of flight. A seagull has long, slim wings to glide swiftly over the water; a buzzard's broad wings and tail mean it can circle while waiting to swoop; the swallow has narrow wings to dart about rapidly, close to the ground, in search of insects; and the pheasant's short, wide wings enable it to flap quickly upward out of the undergrowth.

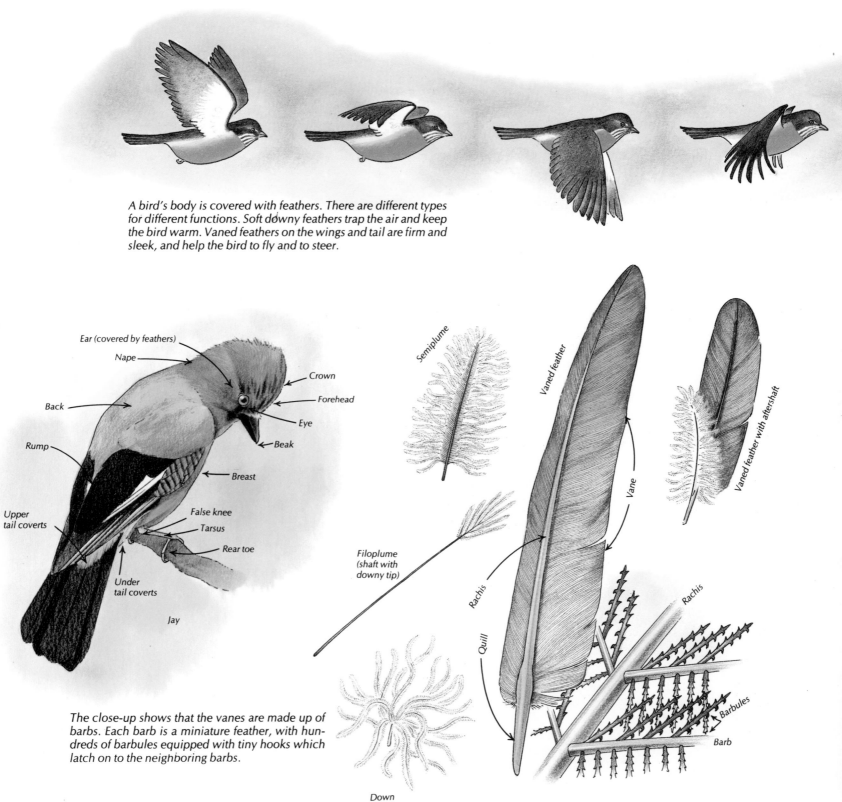

A bird's body is covered with feathers. There are different types for different functions. Soft downy feathers trap the air and keep the bird warm. Vaned feathers on the wings and tail are firm and sleek, and help the bird to fly and to steer.

Ear (covered by feathers)
Nape
Crown
Back
Forehead
Eye
Beak
Rump
Breast
Upper tail coverts
False knee
Tarsus
Rear toe
Under tail coverts

Jay

Semiplume
Vaned feather
Vaned feather with aftershaft
Vane
Filoplume (shaft with downy tip)
Rachis
Quill
Rachis
Barbules
Barb

The close-up shows that the vanes are made up of barbs. Each barb is a miniature feather, with hundreds of barbules equipped with tiny hooks which latch on to the neighboring barbs.

Down

100

Seagull

Buzzard

Swallow

Pheasant

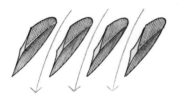

During the upstroke the feathers tilt and separate to offer the minimum of resistance to the air.

Feathers on the upstroke

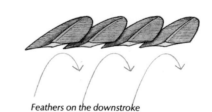

Feathers on the downstroke

During the downstroke they close, overlapping like roof tiles, to give the maximum of push.

Section of a bird's bone

A bird's bones, which are hollow and contain air, are particularly light and strong. Over half its weight is muscle.

Vaned feathers fall into two main groups: flight feathers which propel the bird, and tail feathers which steer its course. The flight feathers border the wings. The primaries are attached to bones which correspond to our hands, and the secondaries to bones which correspond to our arms. Covering the base of the flight feathers are the covert. The steering and stabilizing feathers, which form the tail, are attached to bones which correspond to the lower vertebrae.

Lesser wing coverts

Greater wing coverts

Primaries

Secondaries

Tail feathers

Magpie

101

Flapping Follies

Since the earliest times, people have looked at birds with admiration for their marvelous ability to fly. Soaring through the air, they seemed the freest of creatures.

Many brave inventors tried to build flapping devices, called ornithopters, which would imitate birds' wings, but none of them realized what enormous strength would be needed to propel them, or what skill to guide them. It was many years before the discovery of the secret of how to design aerodynamic wings.

The Italian artist and designer Leonardo da Vinci, for one, drew numerous sketches of ornithopters. Happily none of his ideas were ever really put into practice, for the pilot would surely have crashed.

Sketches by Leonardo da Vinci, about 1500

Later in life, Leonardo studied birds and made many sketches of them. Unfortunately, his drawings were not published until centuries later, and so could not advance aviation.

102

In 1678 a French locksmith named Besnier claimed that he had invented a pair of flapping paddles which he had used to cross rivers and fly over his neighbors' houses. More likely, he used them once and got a cold dunking for it!

In 1781 another Frenchman, Jean Pierre Blanchard, dreamed up this boat, which he hoped to paddle not through water but through air! Fortunately, he suspended his craft from a cord and tested it, and, doubtless disappointed with the results, took the idea no further. Four years later, however, he successfully crossed the Channel by hydrogen balloon.

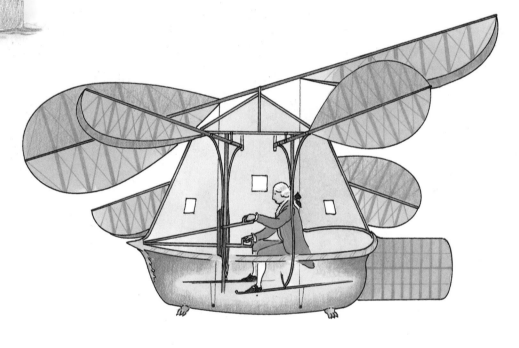

In 1801 a French general named Resnier de Goué built and tested an ornithopter at the age of seventy-two. Lucky to survive the inevitable fall with nothing worse than a broken leg, he told the story until his death ten years later.

On July 9, 1874, a Belgian inventor, Vincent de Groof, attached his ornithopter to a balloon and was towed skyward over London. He cut the cord to begin his flight, and it was the last thing he ever did.

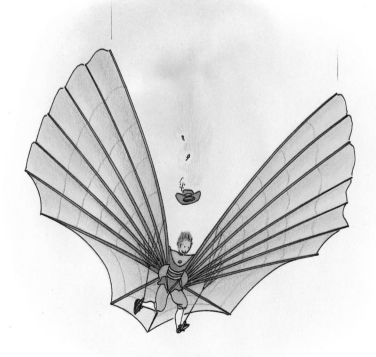

103

Searching for the Secret of Wings

The secret of wings lies in their shape. To be effective, they must cut swiftly through the air. The upper side of a wing is curved in such a way that the air passing over it has further to travel than the air below and is forced to go faster.

This spreads the particles more thinly. The pressure exerted on the wing from above is less than that exerted from below, so the air below the wing literally pushes it upward and keeps it in flight. In truth, wings perform a trick on the air, and the sight of them lifting the heaviest aircraft into the sky is magical.

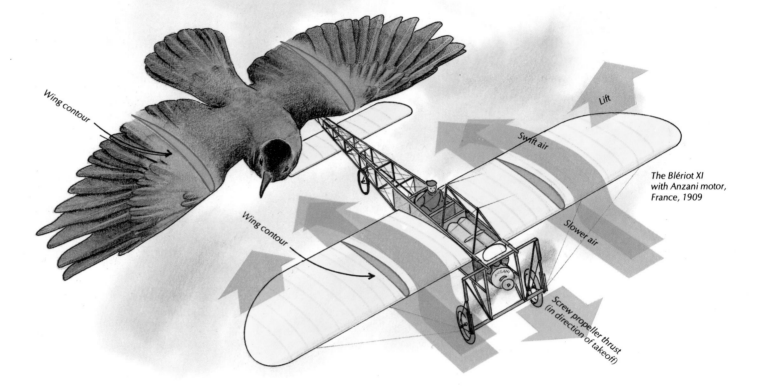

Wing contour

Wing contour

Lift

Swift air

Slower air

Screw propeller thrust (in direction of takeoff)

The Blériot XI with Anzani motor, France, 1909

Fast air

Lift is produced

Cut-off air

To test the secret of wings for yourself, take a sheet of thin, light paper. Hold it so that it is hanging downward, at about the level of your lower lip. Take a deep breath and blow strongly. The wind of your breath reduces the pressure on the outer surface . . . and the sheet begins to rise!

Between 1891 and 1896, after years of study and experiment, the German inventor Otto Lilienthal made a series of long hops and glides which excited the world. Photographs of them were published widely, and inspired others to try their hand at gliding, too. Lilienthal's love of gliding was to cost him his life.

The automobile was invented at the same time as Lilienthal was making his glides. Inside it was the gasoline engine: light but powerful, this was the missing element, enabling aircraft to take to the air at last.

Otto Lilienthal was a German inventor who studied the flight of birds very carefully and realized that the secret did not lie in the flapping of the wings but in their shape. He built several gliders, taking great care over them, and in 1891 propelled himself down the slope of a hill near Berlin and took off in the first successful glide.

The Birth of Powered Flight

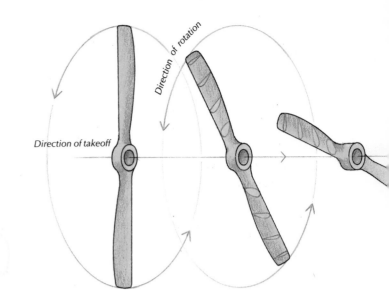

With proper wings, it was possible to build a glider. But to build a powered aircraft, and fly like a bird, was a much larger problem! Birds have very strong muscles to operate their wings, and an airplane, similarly, needs a strong power-plant to propel it through the air.

The first practical aircraft engine, light yet powerful, was derived from the gasoline engine of the newly invented automobile. But to design a complete and practical aircraft from scratch took more than wings and a motor. It took genius. Fortunately the genius was at hand.

Wilbur and Orville Wright

Otto Lilienthal

The Wright brothers were bicycle-builders from Dayton in Ohio. They first became interested in flying when they read an article about Lilienthal's glides in Germany. Like him, they understood that a controlled flight was the only successful one. They experimented with winged kites and gliders, and found that by changing the angle of the wingtips they could keep the craft steady in the wind and bank it from side to side. The technique was to become known as "wing-warping".

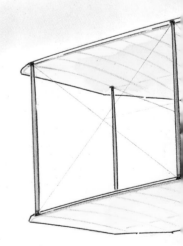

The Wright brothers made many glides on the windy beaches near Kitty Hawk in North Carolina.

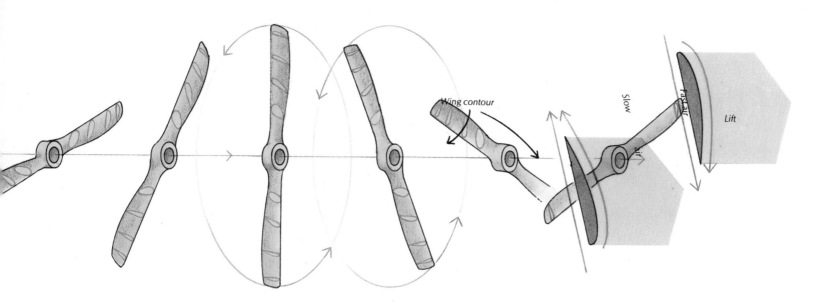

Wing contour

Slow

Lift

In the winter of 1903 the Wright brothers brought to their campsite a craft powered by two pusher propellers. They called their craft the *Flyer*, and took turns trying to fly it. On December 17, they launched it from a trolley running along a rail laid in the sand, into the wind. It was Orville who was aboard when the machine lifted off, dipped and rose, and landed about 120 feet (36 meters) away. They made three more flights, the longest being 852 feet (260 meters), on that historic day.

A wing will lift if air rushes swiftly over its upper surface. If you mount a wing on a peg and make it spin very fast, once again it should lift into the air. A propeller is essentially a pair of spinning wings, lifting themselves up into, and through, the air.

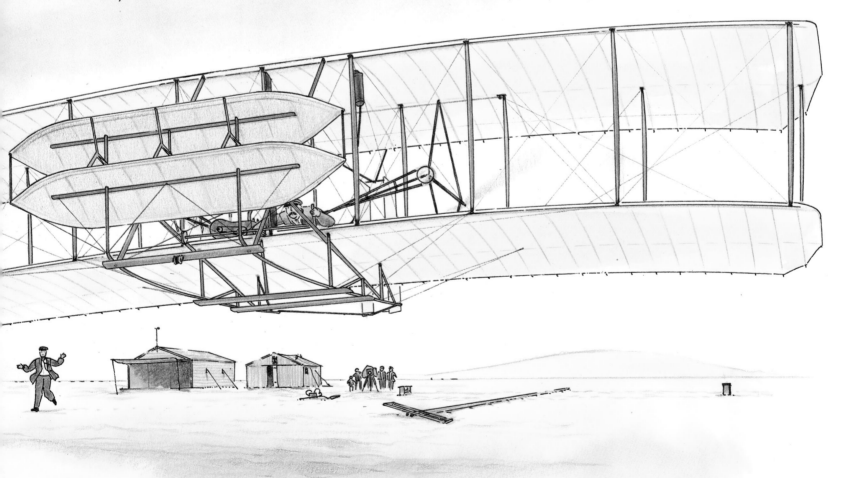

Flying

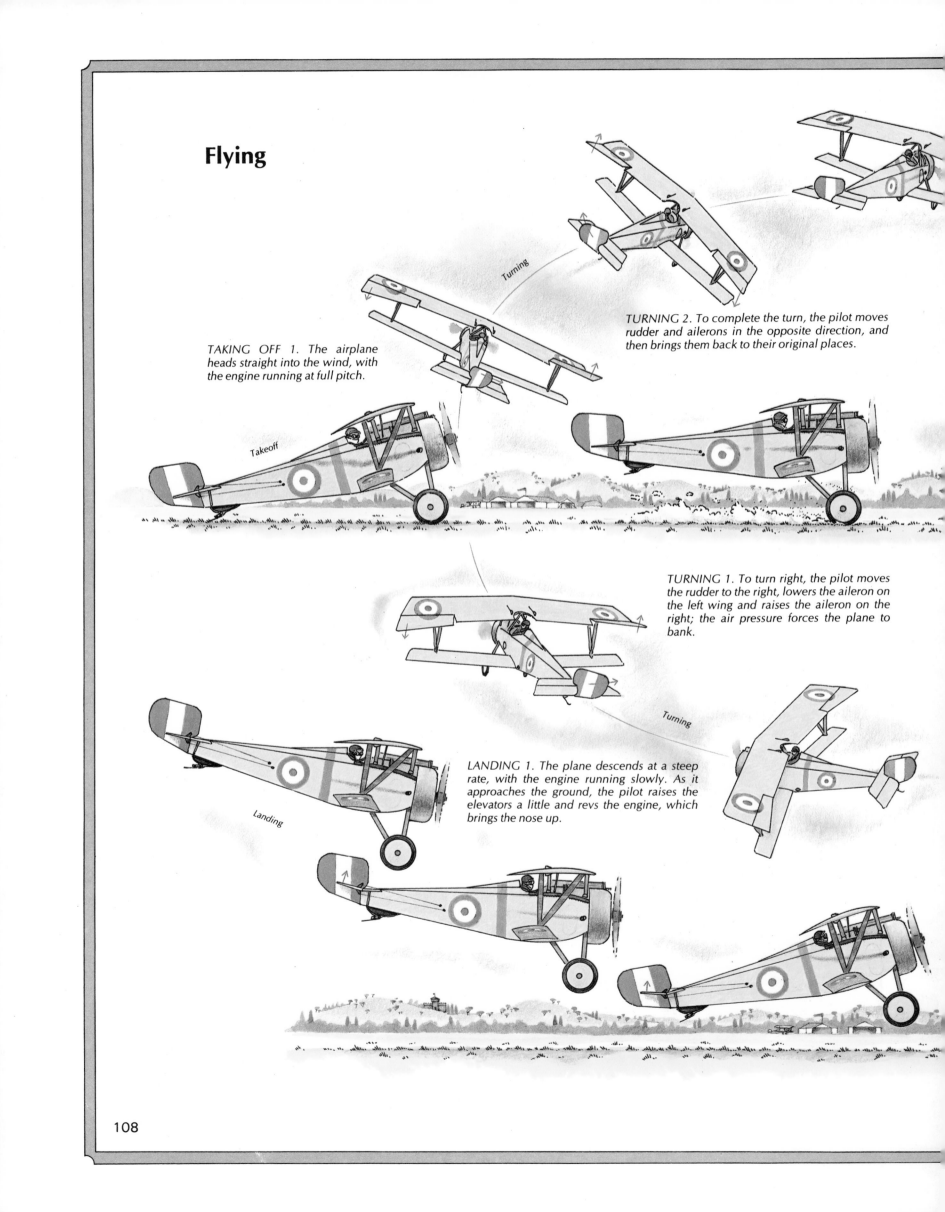

TURNING 2. To complete the turn, the pilot moves rudder and ailerons in the opposite direction, and then brings them back to their original places.

TAKING OFF 1. The airplane heads straight into the wind, with the engine running at full pitch.

Turning

Takeoff

TURNING 1. To turn right, the pilot moves the rudder to the right, lowers the aileron on the left wing and raises the aileron on the right; the air pressure forces the plane to bank.

LANDING 1. The plane descends at a steep rate, with the engine running slowly. As it approaches the ground, the pilot raises the elevators a little and revs the engine, which brings the nose up.

Landing

Turning

108

Of all the Earth's oceans, the Ocean of Air is perhaps the most difficult to sail! Any aircraft is constantly affected by turbulence, buffeting winds and abrupt changes of weather.

Every airplane is equipped with controls, and an experienced pilot can maneuver it with the agility of a bird. The three basic maneuvers are taking off, turning the plane, and landing.

TAKING OFF 2. As the airplane rolls forward quickly, the pilot raises the elevators, pointing the nose skyward, and the plane lifts off.

TAKING OFF 3. The pilot levels off to gain speed, and then gently raises the elevators again; the plane is off and away.

Cockpit

Propeller

Italian military markings

Aileron (enabling the plane to bank)

Engine cowling

Rudder

Fuselage

Tailplane

Tailskid

Elevator

Landing gear

Wooden chock (to wedge the wheels until the plane taxis forward to take off).

This Nieuport Macchi 17 from World War I (1914–18) flew for the Italian Air Force. It is a biplane (so called because the wings are double), with a wooden frame covered by canvas and held together with wire rigging. Today, airplanes are built of steel and aluminum.

LANDING 2. The engine speed is so low that the wings can barely lift the plane, and it drops gently to a three-point landing.

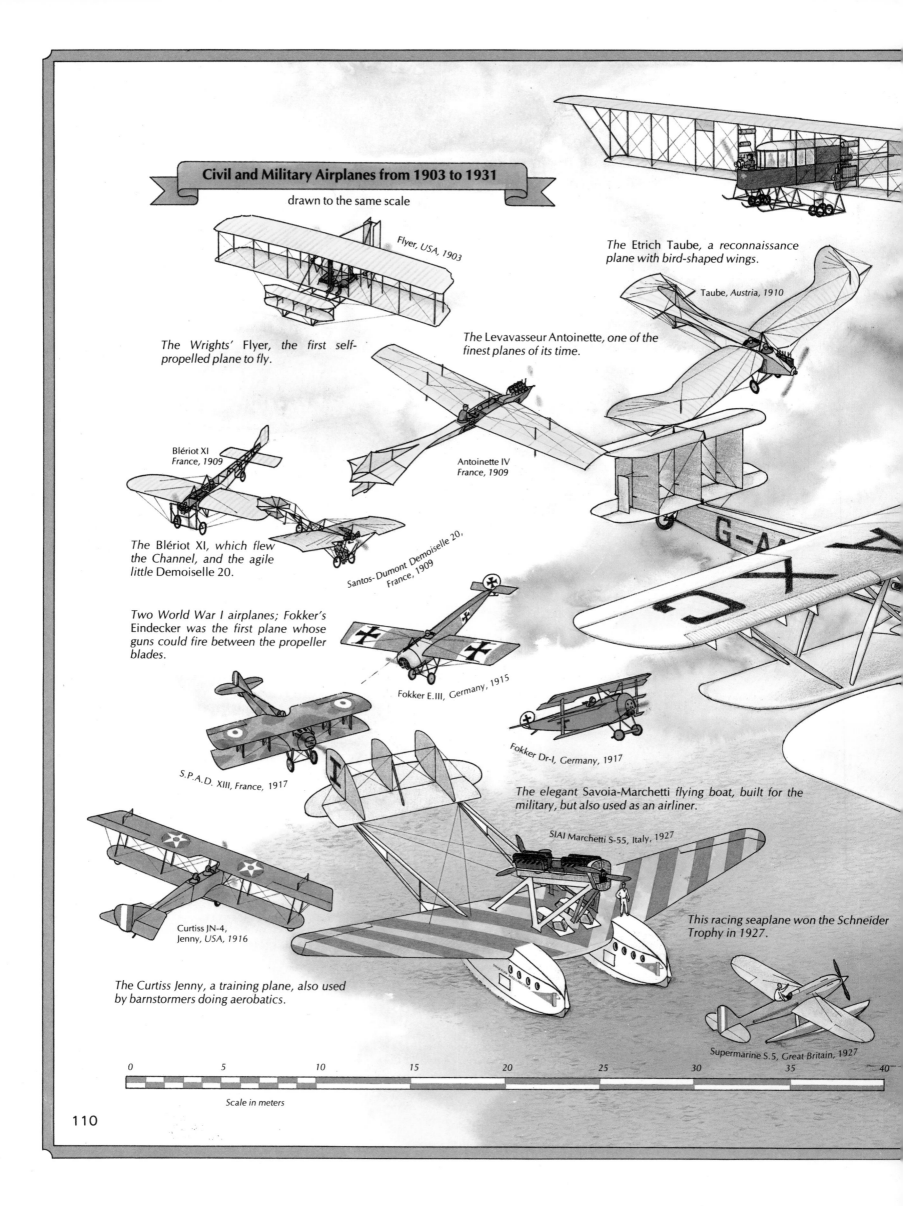

Civil and Military Airplanes from 1903 to 1931

drawn to the same scale

Flyer, USA, 1903

The Wrights' Flyer, the first self-propelled plane to fly.

The Etrich Taube, a reconnaissance plane with bird-shaped wings.

Taube, Austria, 1910

The Levavasseur Antoinette, one of the finest planes of its time.

Blériot XI
France, 1909

Antoinette IV
France, 1909

The Blériot XI, which flew the Channel, and the agile little Demoiselle 20.

Santos-Dumont Demoiselle 20, France, 1909

Two World War I airplanes; Fokker's Eindecker was the first plane whose guns could fire between the propeller blades.

Fokker E.III, Germany, 1915

Fokker Dr-I, Germany, 1917

S.P.A.D. XIII, France, 1917

The elegant Savoia-Marchetti flying boat, built for the military, but also used as an airliner.

SIAI Marchetti S-55, Italy, 1927

Curtiss JN-4, Jenny, USA, 1916

This racing seaplane won the Schneider Trophy in 1927.

The Curtiss Jenny, a training plane, also used by barnstormers doing aerobatics.

Supermarine S.5, Great Britain, 1927

0   5   10   15   20   25   30   35   40

Scale in meters

110

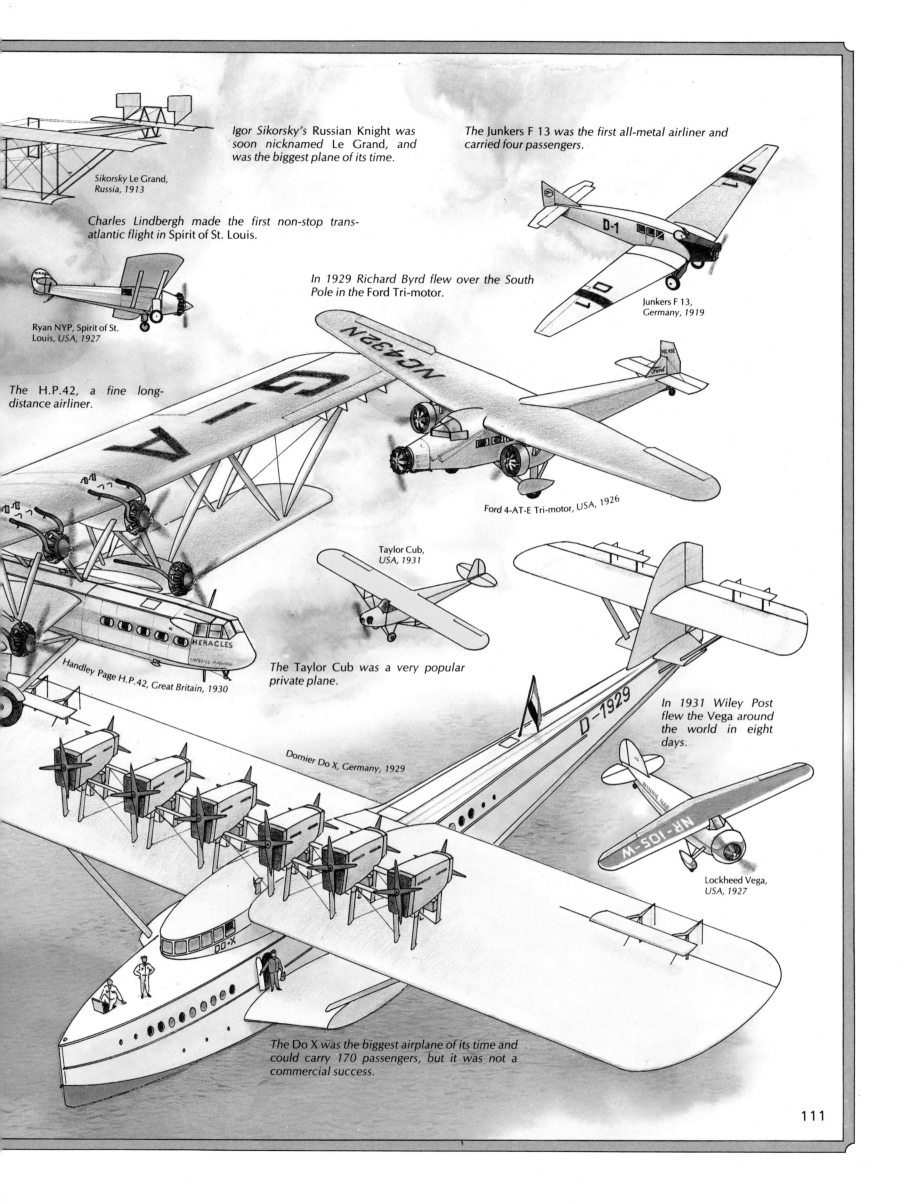

Igor Sikorsky's Russian Knight *was soon nicknamed* Le Grand, *and was the biggest plane of its time.*

Sikorsky Le Grand, Russia, 1913

The Junkers F 13 *was the first all-metal airliner and carried four passengers.*

Charles Lindbergh *made the first non-stop transatlantic flight in* Spirit of St. Louis.

Ryan NYP, Spirit of St. Louis, USA, 1927

In 1929 Richard Byrd *flew over the South Pole in the Ford Tri-motor.*

Junkers F 13, Germany, 1919

The H.P.42, *a fine long-distance airliner.*

Ford 4-AT-E Tri-motor, USA, 1926

Taylor Cub, USA, 1931

Handley Page H.P.42, Great Britain, 1930

The Taylor Cub *was a very popular private plane.*

In 1931 Wiley Post *flew the Vega around the world in eight days.*

Dornier Do X, Germany, 1929

Lockheed Vega, USA, 1927

The Do X *was the biggest airplane of its time and could carry 170 passengers, but it was not a commercial success.*

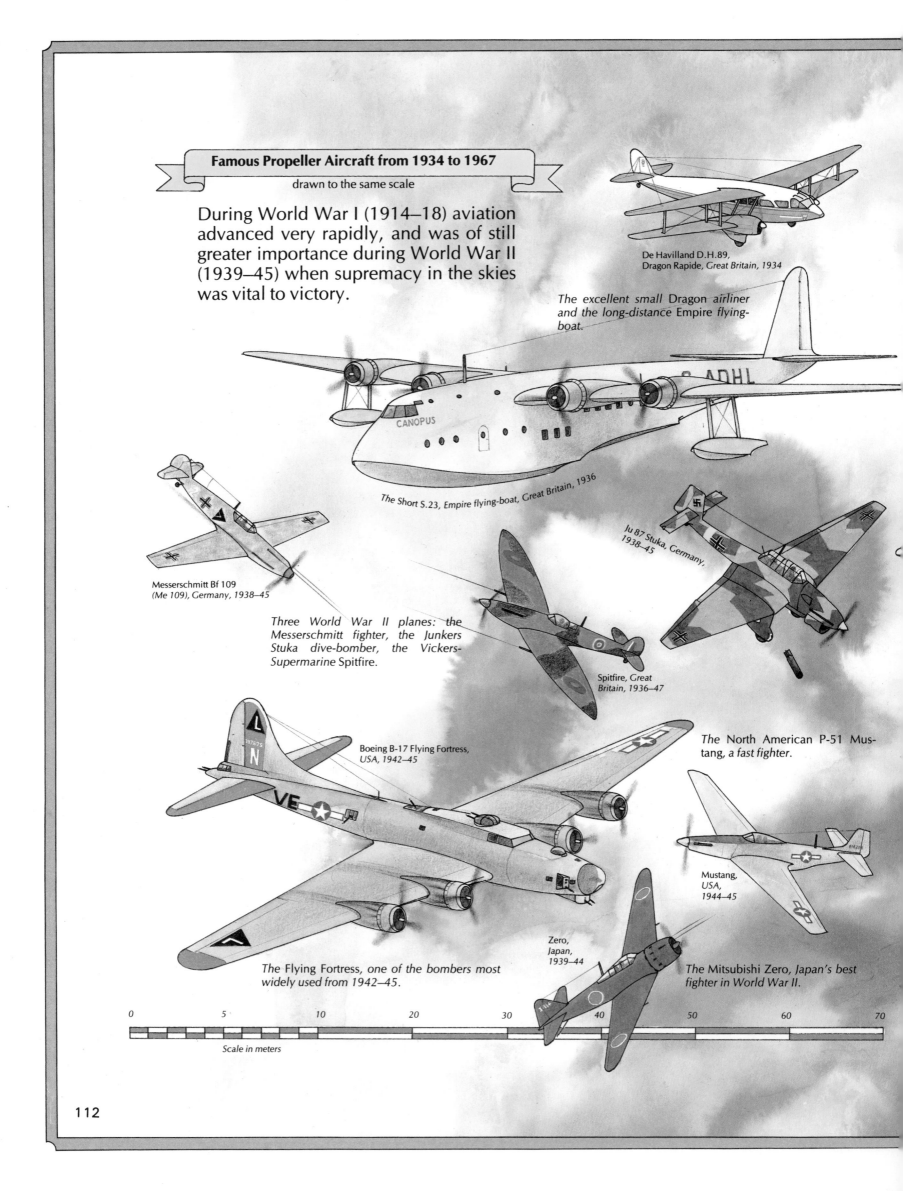

Famous Propeller Aircraft from 1934 to 1967

drawn to the same scale

During World War I (1914–18) aviation advanced very rapidly, and was of still greater importance during World War II (1939–45) when supremacy in the skies was vital to victory.

De Havilland D.H.89, Dragon Rapide, Great Britain, 1934

The excellent small Dragon airliner and the long-distance Empire flying-boat.

CANOPUS

The Short S.23, Empire flying-boat, Great Britain, 1936

Ju 87 Stuka, Germany, 1938–45

Messerschmitt Bf 109 (Me 109), Germany, 1938–45

Three World War II planes: the Messerschmitt fighter, the Junkers Stuka dive-bomber, the Vickers-Supermarine Spitfire.

Spitfire, Great Britain, 1936–47

Boeing B-17 Flying Fortress, USA, 1942–45

The North American P-51 Mustang, a fast fighter.

Mustang, USA, 1944–45

Zero, Japan, 1939–44

The Flying Fortress, one of the bombers most widely used from 1942–45.

The Mitsubishi Zero, Japan's best fighter in World War II.

| 0 | 5 | 10 | 20 | 30 | 40 | 50 | 60 | 70 |

Scale in meters

Douglas DC-3, *USA, 1935–45*

The Douglas DC-3 *was perhaps the most famous and widely used airplane ever built; in military use it was known popularly as the Dakota (C-47).*

The Clippers *were the biggest flying-boats used by Pan American Airways on long-distance routes.*

Boeing 314, *Yankee Clipper, USA, 1939*

The Mosquito, *a wood-and-canvas bomber whose performance was so good that some versions carried no defense armament.*

De Havilland Mosquito, *Great Britain, 1941–45*

Modified versions of the rugged and reliable Lancaster *bomber were used on the famous "Dambusters" wartime raid in 1943.*

Avro Lancaster, *Great Britain, 1941–46*

The Skyvan *is used by many airlines for short hauls, carrying passengers or cargo.*

Short Skyvan, *Great Britain, 1967*

The Cessna 150, *one of the world's most popular light aircraft.*

Cessna 150, *USA, 1957*

Winged seed-pod spiraling gently to the ground

Toy spinner

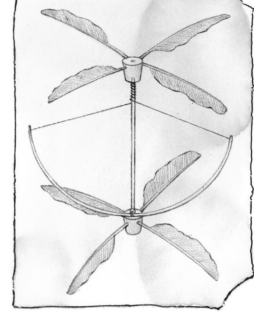

Drawing of a toy rotor designed by George Cayley in 1809

Helicopters

A helicopter has wings, too, but with a difference. They are active, spinning as a rotor above the craft, and generating their own lift. This makes a helicopter uniquely maneuverable. It can hover overhead, slide through the air in any direction, and take off from or land in the most inaccessible spots.

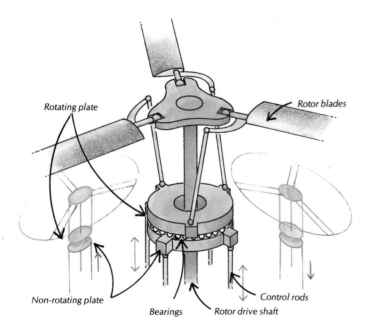

Rotating plate

Rotor blades

Non-rotating plate

Bearings

Rotor drive shaft

Control rods

The helicopter owes its maneuverability to its swashplate. Located below the rotor, and connected by rods to the controls, it can tilt the rotor disc to any angle, enabling the craft to slide in the desired direction. The upper plate spins with the rotor, the lower does not.

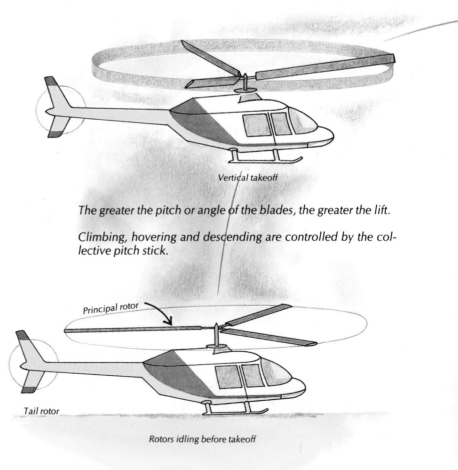

Vertical takeoff

The greater the pitch or angle of the blades, the greater the lift.

Climbing, hovering and descending are controlled by the collective pitch stick.

Principal rotor

Tail rotor

Rotors idling before takeoff

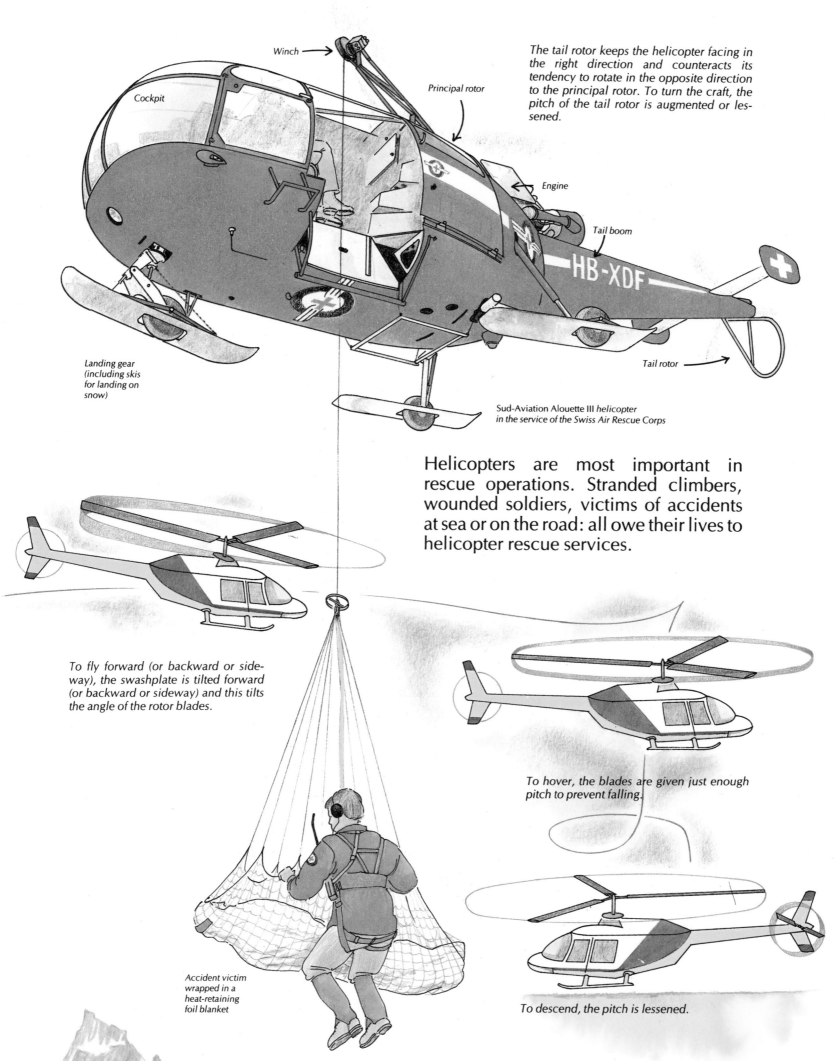

Winch →

Cockpit

Principal rotor

The tail rotor keeps the helicopter facing in the right direction and counteracts its tendency to rotate in the opposite direction to the principal rotor. To turn the craft, the pitch of the tail rotor is augmented or lessened.

Engine

Tail boom

HB-XDF

Landing gear (including skis for landing on snow)

Tail rotor →

Sud-Aviation Alouette III *helicopter in the service of the Swiss Air Rescue Corps*

Helicopters are most important in rescue operations. Stranded climbers, wounded soldiers, victims of accidents at sea or on the road: all owe their lives to helicopter rescue services.

To fly forward (or backward or sideway), the swashplate is tilted forward (or backward or sideway) and this tilts the angle of the rotor blades.

To hover, the blades are given just enough pitch to prevent falling.

Accident victim wrapped in a heat-retaining foil blanket

To descend, the pitch is lessened.

Jets

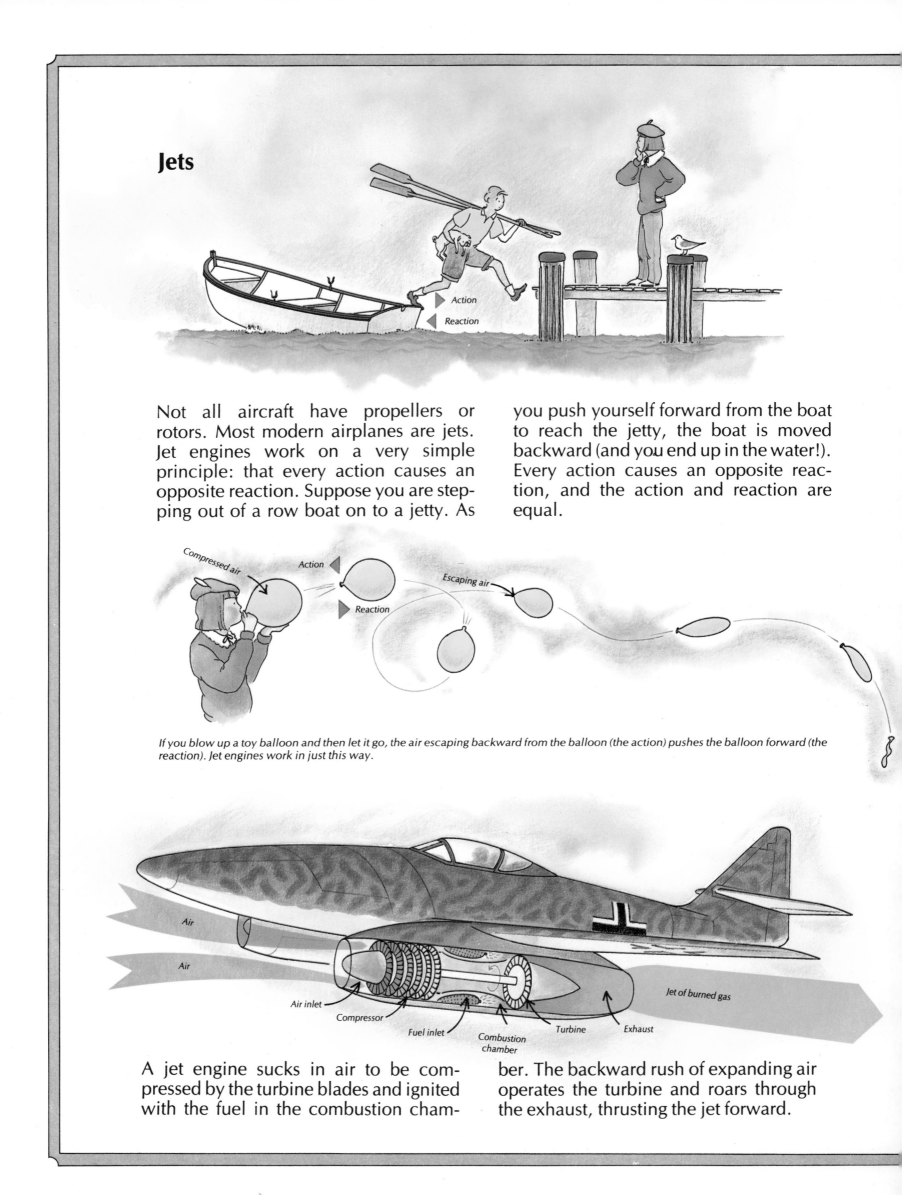

Not all aircraft have propellers or rotors. Most modern airplanes are jets. Jet engines work on a very simple principle: that every action causes an opposite reaction. Suppose you are stepping out of a row boat on to a jetty. As you push yourself forward from the boat to reach the jetty, the boat is moved backward (and you end up in the water!). Every action causes an opposite reaction, and the action and reaction are equal.

If you blow up a toy balloon and then let it go, the air escaping backward from the balloon (the action) pushes the balloon forward (the reaction). Jet engines work in just this way.

A jet engine sucks in air to be compressed by the turbine blades and ignited with the fuel in the combustion chamber. The backward rush of expanding air operates the turbine and roars through the exhaust, thrusting the jet forward.

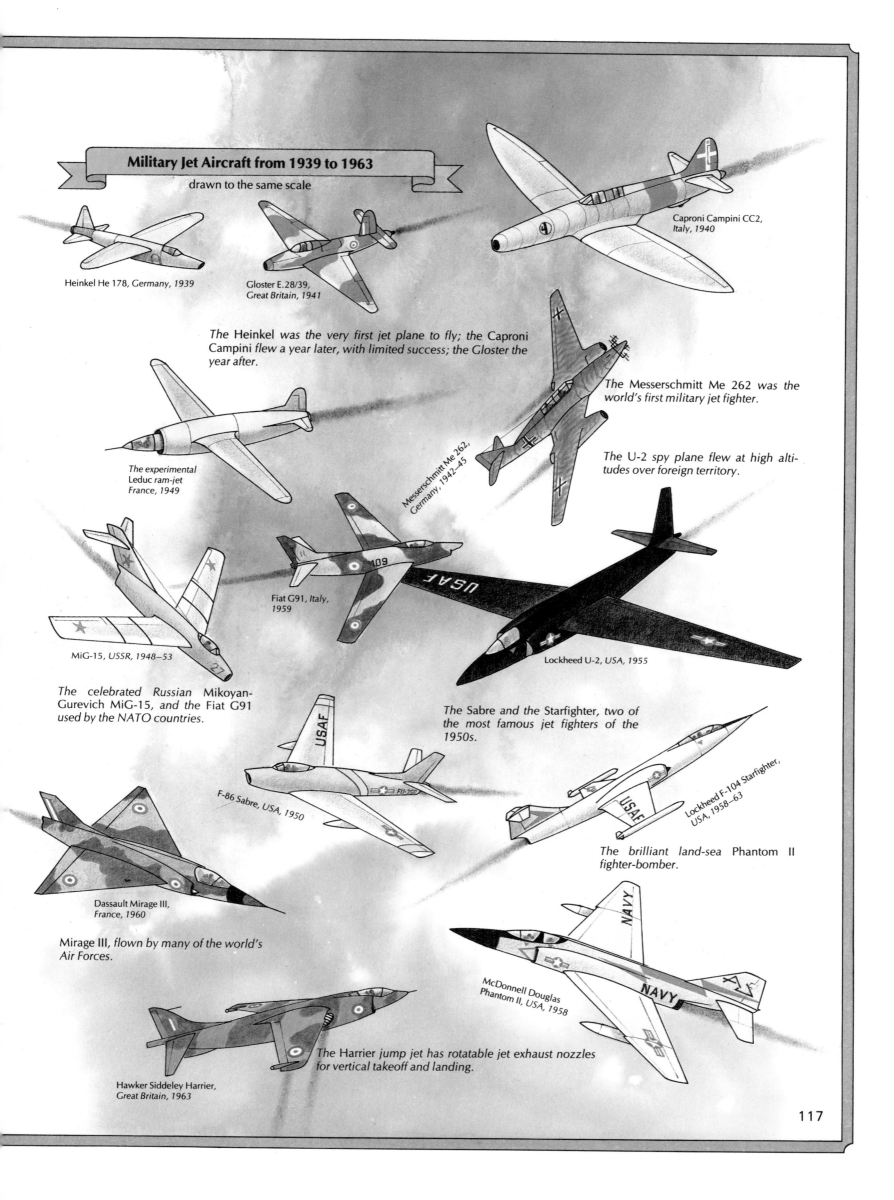

Military Jet Aircraft from 1939 to 1963

drawn to the same scale

Heinkel He 178, Germany, 1939

Gloster E.28/39,
Great Britain, 1941

Caproni Campini CC2,
Italy, 1940

The Heinkel *was the very first jet plane to fly; the Caproni Campini flew a year later, with limited success; the Gloster the year after.*

The experimental
Leduc ram-jet
France, 1949

Messerschmitt Me 262,
Germany, 1942–45

The Messerschmitt Me 262 *was the world's first military jet fighter.*

The U-2 *spy plane flew at high altitudes over foreign territory.*

Fiat G91, Italy,
1959

MiG-15, USSR, 1948–53

Lockheed U-2, USA, 1955

The celebrated Russian Mikoyan-Gurevich MiG-15, *and the Fiat G91 used by the NATO countries.*

The Sabre *and the* Starfighter, *two of the most famous jet fighters of the 1950s.*

F-86 Sabre, USA, 1950

Lockheed F-104 Starfighter,
USA, 1958–63

The brilliant land-sea Phantom II fighter-bomber.

Dassault Mirage III,
France, 1960

Mirage III, *flown by many of the world's Air Forces.*

McDonnell Douglas
Phantom II, USA, 1958

The Harrier *jump jet has rotatable jet exhaust nozzles for vertical takeoff and landing.*

Hawker Siddeley Harrier,
Great Britain, 1963

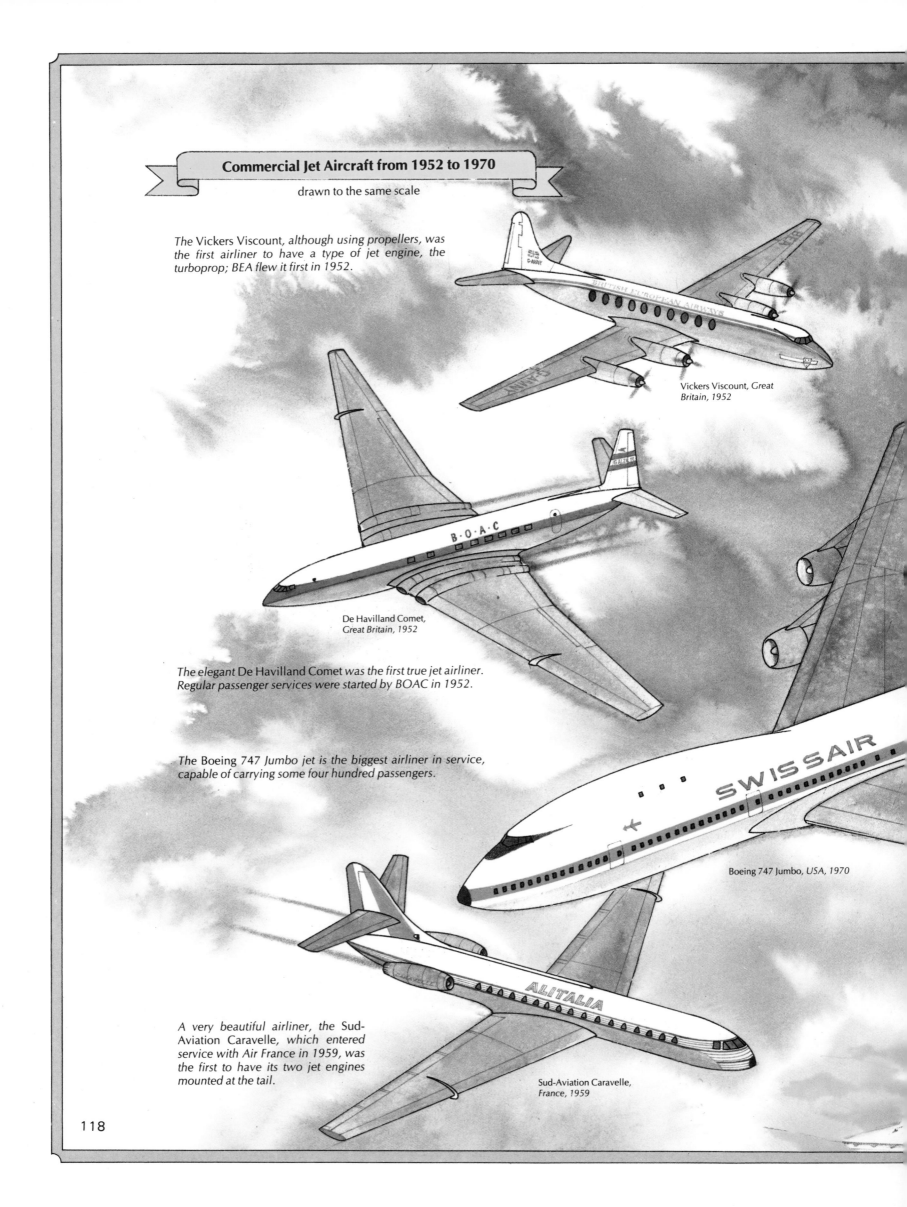

Commercial Jet Aircraft from 1952 to 1970

drawn to the same scale

The Vickers Viscount, *although using propellers, was the first airliner to have a type of jet engine, the turboprop; BEA flew it first in 1952.*

Vickers Viscount, *Great Britain, 1952*

De Havilland Comet, *Great Britain, 1952*

The elegant De Havilland Comet *was the first true jet airliner. Regular passenger services were started by BOAC in 1952.*

The Boeing 747 *Jumbo jet is the biggest airliner in service, capable of carrying some four hundred passengers.*

Boeing 747 Jumbo, *USA, 1970*

A very beautiful airliner, the Sud-Aviation Caravelle, *which entered service with Air France in 1959, was the first to have its two jet engines mounted at the tail.*

Sud-Aviation Caravelle, *France, 1959*

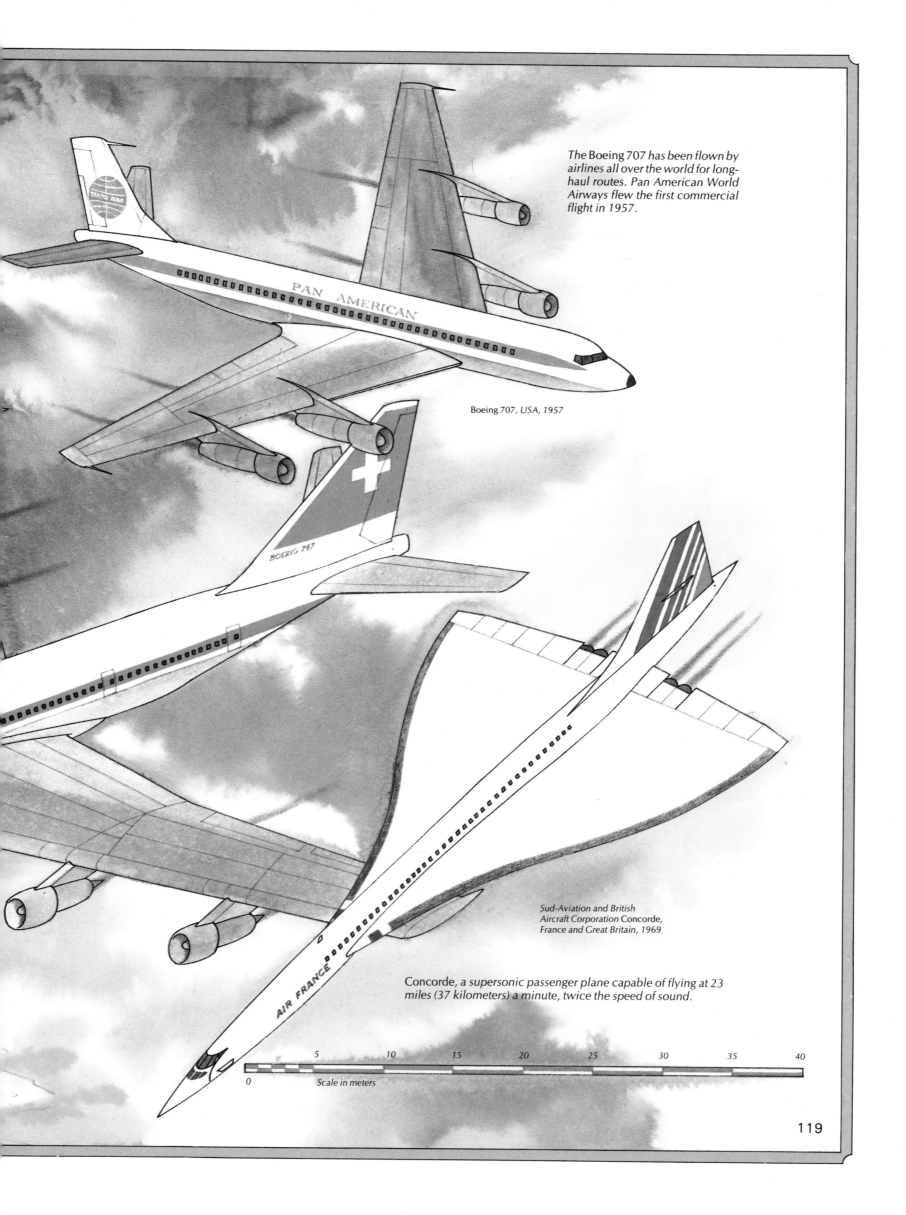

The Boeing 707 has been flown by airlines all over the world for long-haul routes. Pan American World Airways flew the first commercial flight in 1957.

Boeing 707, USA, 1957

Sud-Aviation and British Aircraft Corporation Concorde, France and Great Britain, 1969

Concorde, a supersonic passenger plane capable of flying at 23 miles (37 kilometers) a minute, twice the speed of sound.

0   5   10   15   20   25   30   35   40
Scale in meters

How Grandad Used to Fly . . .

Air travel has changed tremendously since the first airplanes took to the air, at the start of the century. The first fliers used a flat grassy field for takeoff and landing. They didn't go too far from home, and they flew in fair weather so that they could spot landmarks below and check their position by a road map. But at night, or over the sea, or in fog, pilots needed a navigation system. Dead reckoning was the simplest means of finding the way.

The Etrich Taube, 1910

0 10 20 30 40 50 60 70 80 90 100 110 120 130 140 *Miles*

Lindbergh's Spirit of St. Louis 1927

Compass

Map

If you know your position at, say, 8 o'clock, and fly due east at 140 miles per hour, keeping to a compass heading of 90°, at 9 o'clock you should be 140 miles due east of your original position; and so you can plot a course from point to point. The system isn't foolproof as it doesn't allow for cross-winds pushing you off course, but in 1927 Lindbergh found his way across the Atlantic by dead reckoning alone.

The invention of radio was an enormous help; with the aid of a loop aerial, you could pick up radio beams and vary their intensity.

By lining up the transmitter with the angle of the aerial, you knew the line along which the plane was flying, and by lining up a second transmitter you had your exact position.

Loop aerial

Radio operator

SIAI Marchetti S.M.

Radio transmitter

120

This is an airport fifty years ago. The airplane is a Fokker F-VIIa monoplane of 1931, which carried between eight and ten passengers, cruised at 100–15 mph (165–85 kmh) and could fly about 500 miles (800 kilometers) without refueling. The cabin was tiny, with lightweight wicker chairs, and big windows gave a good view of the ground, which was never very far below. A flight attendant served light refreshments and gave you chewing gum or barley sugar to keep your ears from popping.

The airport was a flat grassy field, which was large enough for airplanes to take off or land into the wind, from whichever direction it was blowing. The windsock showed the wind's direction. The field was lined with hangars, where the aircraft were stored and repaired. The airport kept in touch with the pilots thanks to radio.

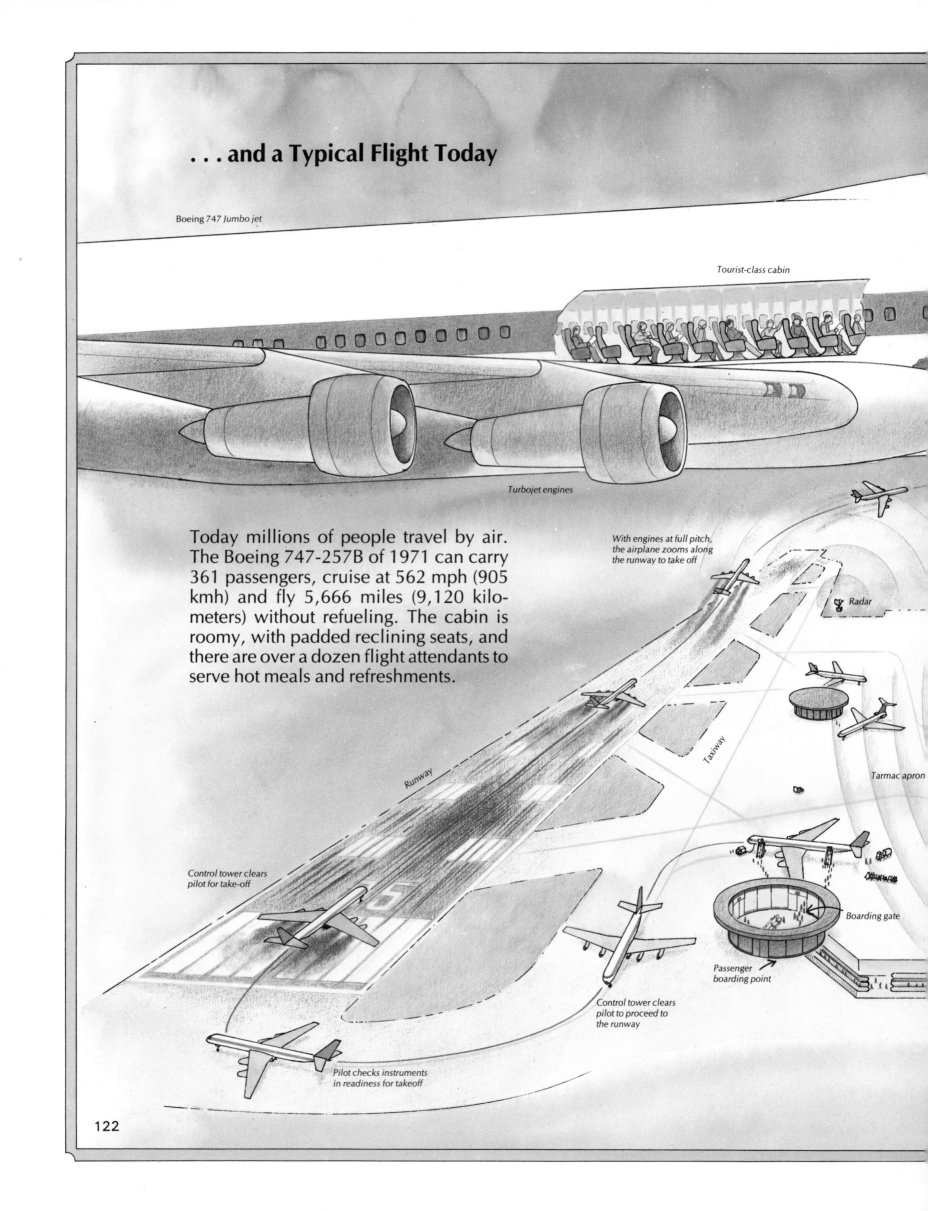

...and a Typical Flight Today

Boeing 747 Jumbo jet

Tourist-class cabin

Turbojet engines

Today millions of people travel by air. The Boeing 747-257B of 1971 can carry 361 passengers, cruise at 562 mph (905 kmh) and fly 5,666 miles (9,120 kilometers) without refueling. The cabin is roomy, with padded reclining seats, and there are over a dozen flight attendants to serve hot meals and refreshments.

With engines at full pitch, the airplane zooms along the runway to take off

Radar

Taxiway

Tarmac apron

Runway

Control tower clears pilot for take-off

Boarding gate

Passenger boarding point

Control tower clears pilot to proceed to the runway

Pilot checks instruments in readiness for takeoff

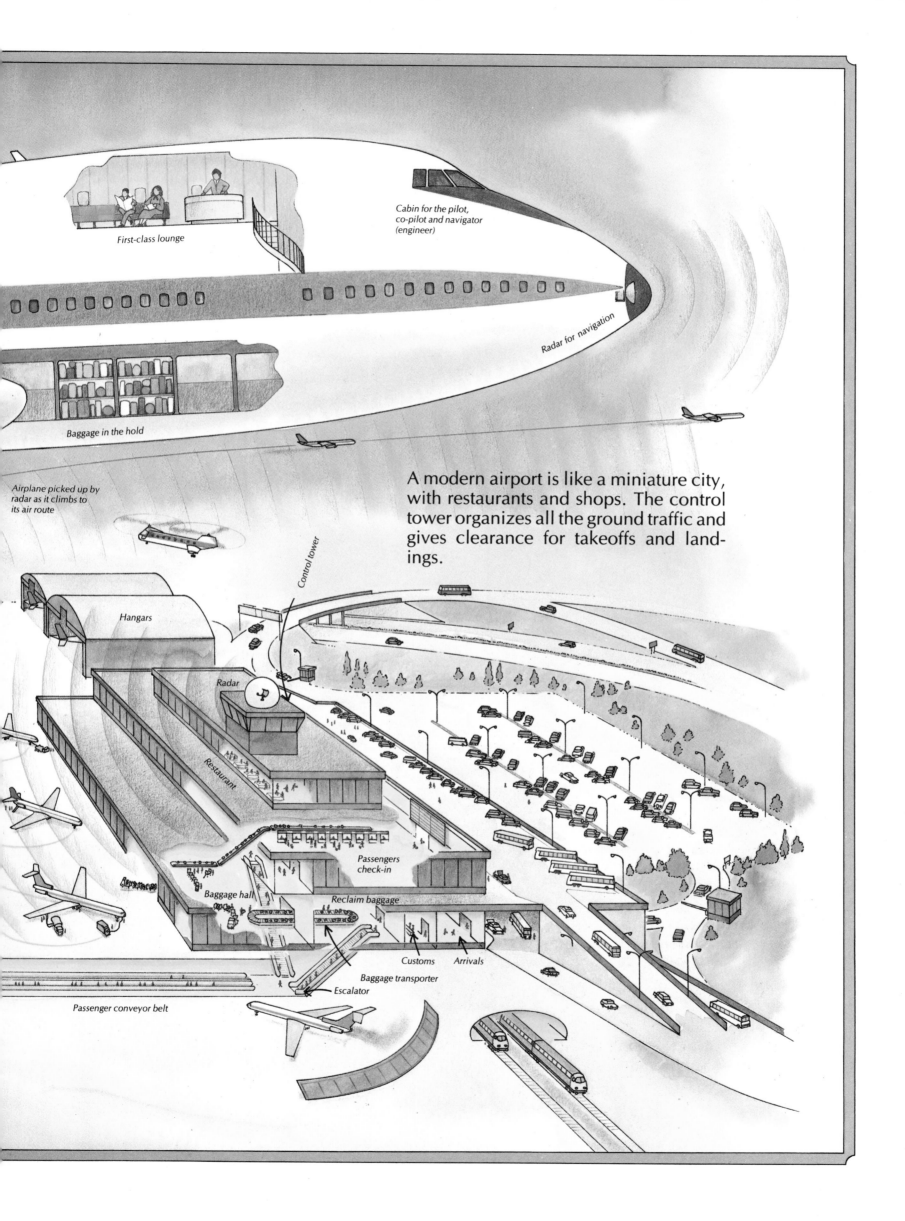

First-class lounge

Cabin for the pilot, co-pilot and navigator (engineer)

Radar for navigation

Baggage in the hold

Airplane picked up by radar as it climbs to its air route

A modern airport is like a miniature city, with restaurants and shops. The control tower organizes all the ground traffic and gives clearance for takeoffs and landings.

Control tower

Hangars

Radar

Restaurant

Passengers check-in

Baggage hall

Reclaim baggage

Customs

Arrivals

Baggage transporter

Escalator

Passenger conveyor belt

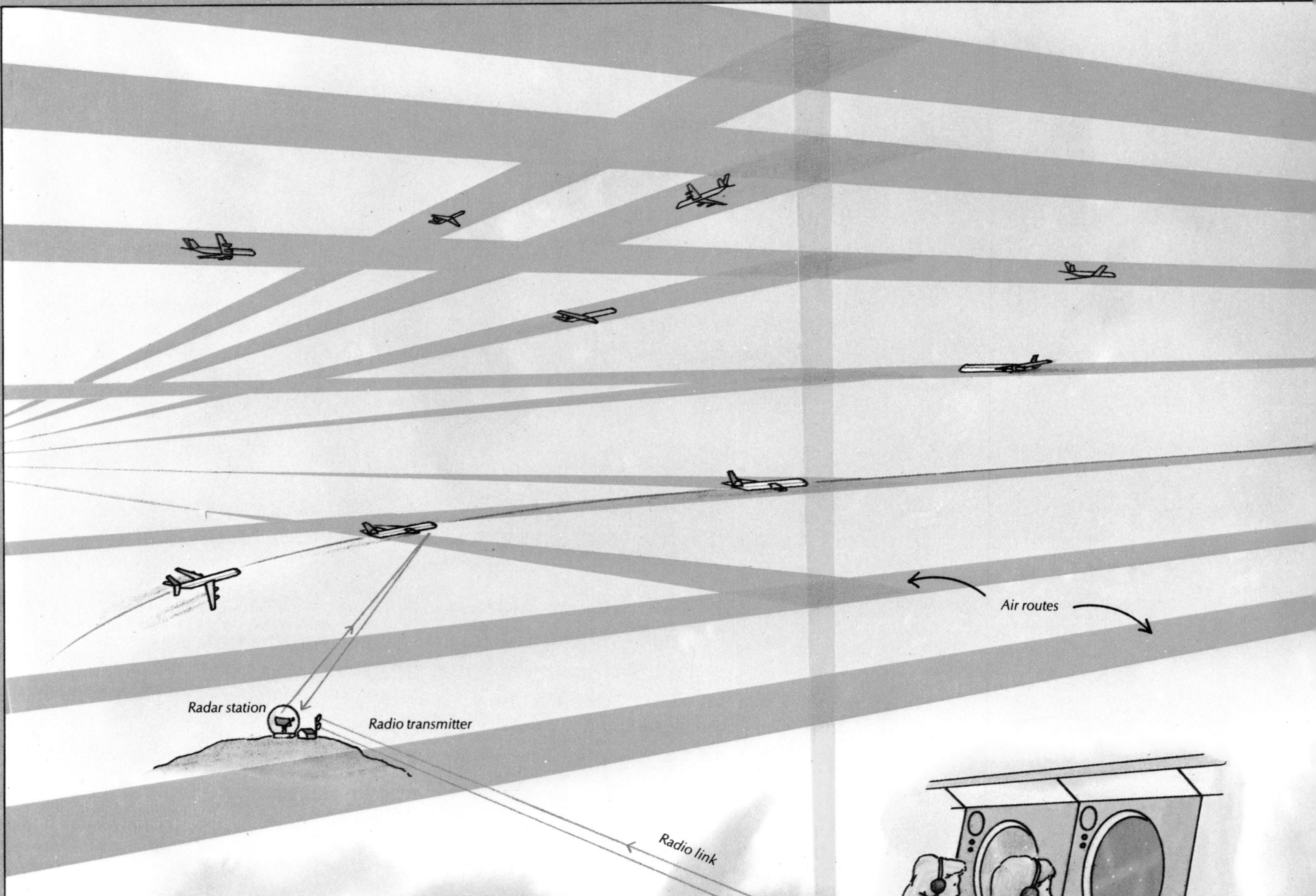

Air routes

Radar station   Radio transmitter

Radio link

The Highways of the Sky

With so many airplanes in the sky today, their greatest problem is to keep out of each other's way. They travel along air routes, or corridors, in the sky, each route being about 11 miles (18 kilometers) wide and 1,000 feet (300 meters) above or below any other, marked by radio beacons at the intersections. The Earth is divided up into regions under air traffic control centers, and every airplane, wherever in the world it may be, is in constant touch with an air traffic controller, who uses radar to track the aircraft overhead, tells the pilots when to change course, and keeps the planes a safe distance apart. Many airports use Instrument Landing System (ILS) transmitters to feed the correct approach path to the instruments in the cockpit, so that landing is automated. Flying today is done largely from the ground.

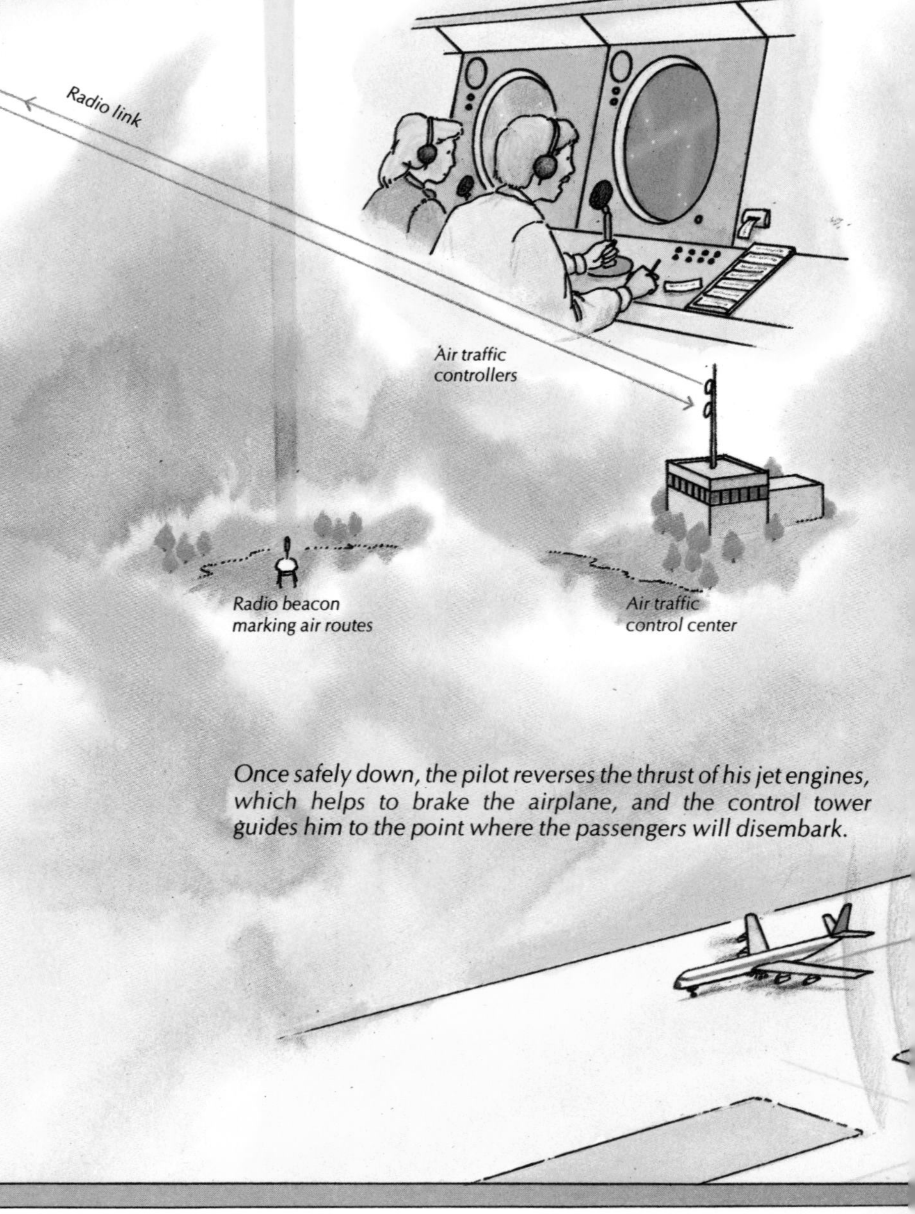

Air traffic controllers

Radio beacon marking air routes

Air traffic control center

Once safely down, the pilot reverses the thrust of his jet engines, which helps to brake the airplane, and the control tower guides him to the point where the passengers will disembark.

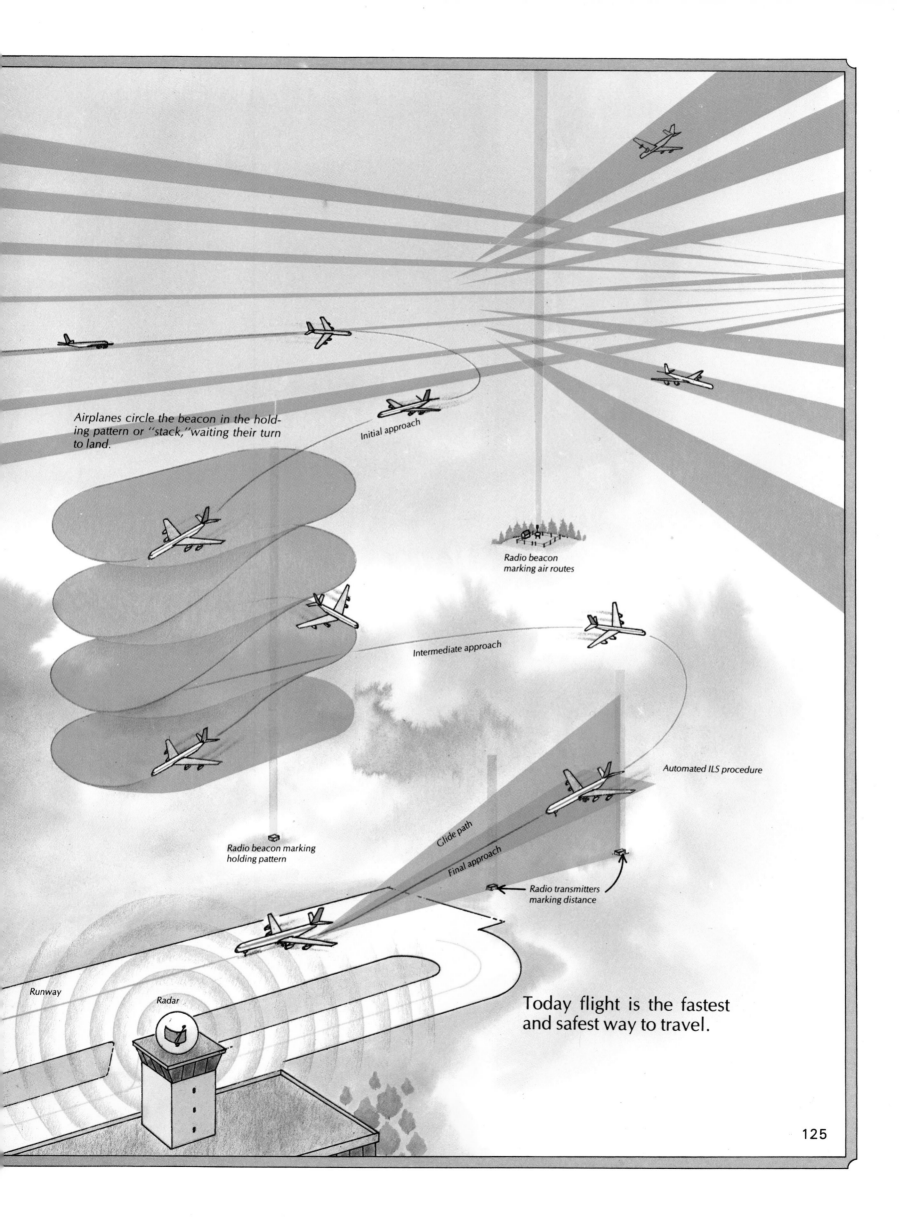

Airplanes circle the beacon in the holding pattern or "stack," waiting their turn to land.

Initial approach

Radio beacon marking air routes

Intermediate approach

Radio beacon marking holding pattern

Glide path

Final approach

Automated ILS procedure

Radio transmitters marking distance

Runway

Radar

Today flight is the fastest and safest way to travel.